BEYOND CORPORATE RESPONSIBILITY

The New Organizational Consciousness

"Beyond Corporate Responsibility: The New Organizational Consciousness" challenges managers to go beyond adopting individual practices such as philanthropy to address social and environmental issues. *Corporate social responsibility (CSR) requires managers to think beyond the boundaries of their organization. As the world becomes more interconnected and social and environmental challenges increase, society and governments will demand businesses show greater leadership for a sustainable future. Chris Caldwell's book is a must read for managers who seek to employ CSR as a means to transition their business to a solution-oriented organization whereby employees are engaged to work together to not only increase the wellbeing of the organization but also the wellbeing of the social and environmental ecosystem that feeds it."*

Irene Henriques
Professor of Sustainability and Economics,
Schulich School of Business, York University

"Chris Caldwell focuses on the essential role of interpersonal relationships within corporate structures to enhance the vitally essential paradigm shifts inherent in the movement towards a sustainable economy and the role that corporations must play."

Dr. Mark Leith
Clinical Teacher, Department of Psychiatry,
University of Toronto,
Author 'Problem Solving Psychotherapy'

"Caldwell shows that an enterprise embracing higher purpose is not making a sustainability sacrifice; it is gaining a sustainability advantage. Social and ecosystems related purposes become the energy source for the economic purpose of a company. B Corps already understand this. This book helps others see the light before their competitors do."

Bob Willard, Author 'The Sustainability
Advantage', Speaker and certified B Corp.

"Managers continuously strive to communicate effectively and influence colleagues to promote their message. Caldwell helps show a way to inspire confidence, win trust and bring a positive message when engaging business and community for social and environmental benefits. Developing your CSR team in ways Caldwell suggests will improve what stakeholders think of your ideas, plans, and improve your entire organization, bringing more respect and credence to you as a leader when you communicate a CSR imperative."

Mark Bowden
Fortune 500 Consultant, Speaker and
Author 'Winning Body Language'

BEYOND CORPORATE RESPONSIBILITY

The New Organizational Consciousness

ENABLING YOUR ORGANIZATION TO REACH ITS
HIGHEST POTENTIAL FOR A SUSTAINABLE
FUTURE

CHRISTOPHER CALDWELL

TIVERO COMMUNICATIONS LTD.

CONTENTS

FOREWORD

A profound change in humanity is occurring. Right now, a rising in consciousness matched only by times of great upheaval and significance in our history is taking place. This period of enlightenment is paradoxically marked by social unrest, a shedding of light on long standing corruption and unfair practices, and growing awareness of ecosystem degradation attributed to our lifestyles - yet the future remains ours to create.

To the enlightened managers and captains of business, the world needs you badly. Humanity is in a new techno-science age in which there is no turning back. Change is happening so swiftly and we have yet to meet the same rate of change in social and environmental progress. We require not specialities, but breadth of scope and education, to bring compassion to our institutions, business and communities. As E.O. Wilson read at a delivery for a TED conference, "Political leaders need at least a modest degree of scientific literacy, which most badly lack today…it would be better for all if they prepared before entering office rather than learning on the job."

Is it too hard to believe that if managers acted as social agents of positive change by empowering their fellow employees by raising the consciousness of the organization, that prosperity and social benefits will follow? Research shows that empowering people on psychic, social and creative levels results in greater productivity and health. This translates directly to better development for the organization. So why are not more organizations taking heed?

The corporate sector has suffered in the wake of scandals, lay-offs and pay-offs underscored by contempt of the working class and a suicidal disposition or ignorance for the social and environmental conditions in which business is done. Excuses range from unsound business cases and affordability to lack of resources or ability to adapt strategy. Communities appear to be left on their own in an age of austerity, as governments, CEOs and lobbyists march into the sunset, people are looking for leaders to come forward and lend authenticity to a much needed sustainability movement, to unite communities and take responsibility for the impacts that we all have a hand in creating. No one can profit in an unsustainable world.

Society is showing the impacts of an exploited planet and exploited people. The poor are getting poorer and the rich, richer, and big business and taxation has become the mechanism for this resource transfer. Wealth in the new paradigm will include health and quality of relationships – the roots of real happiness as many studies now show. And in our rushed quest for happiness, we feel we have no time, that we have devoted ourselves to one more turn of the machine for one more day and do not stop to think if our efforts are squandered or helpful in creating a better society. If we chose, we could create business that does not have a dead end, that offers light at the end of the tunnel and works hand in hand with natural processes and the stakeholder communities. But this will take resolve and an open mind and heart.

The media does its best to offer images of success while Nero plays and Rome falls. With all the distractions it becomes almost impossible to be part of a movement in our own backyards. The use of technology for socialization shows how far removed we are from each other. With a click we can feel like we participated in some sort of advance toward progress for the cause of the day, without even leaving our sofas. We can then forget about the children in other parts of the globe going hungry, indeed in our own cities. Urbanization offers air conditioned malls and underground walkways, we have no need to expose ourselves to nature or the lack thereof. Now, even our man-made environments lack the ethic of building spaces for public use and natural processes.

In this age of globalization, we have lost representation and ability to participate in the evolution of our own well being. Governments are slow and bulky and when they act, they all too often take the sides of the corporate lobbyists. Celebrity businessmen often speak to others of working hard to get ahead, but our best examples show hints of corruption, tax evasion and off-shore banking – ethical business has no soil in which to root itself and thus it is up to us to bring good business to the forefront and celebrate those whose best efforts make a difference.

The fear of commitment to a higher ideal can be strong in an age of insecurity but not inevitable. Workplace cultures are framed for continuance and obedience but the hunger for participation and interaction is a primary attribute of a new generation of graduates. They may find themselves frustrated by the monotony of loveless labour, unable to subvert and curb their talents and desire for progress, they leave or lose vitality, lost to the organization as well. To not make change because we lack the courage would be a disappointing end to our species. Growth comes from exploration and ingenuity, the drivers of business – qualities that need to be embedded in thinking, work processes and daily life. We face threats everyday and routinely deal with them, some natural, most man-made, all of them a chance to learn and grow. Fear of change manifests itself in the clutter humanity is accumulating, full closets, garages, and landfills, unfinished projects, squandered resources, and neglected relationships. Our laziness to excel as people is proportionate with our lack of sustainability. Everywhere we search for a quick and easy cure to our condition when we should be preventing disease in the first place.

With everything happening in the world today, there are signs of renewal - a renaissance of waking grass roots citizenry, startups and innovators. This is where I am pinning my hopes for a bright future. You see the excitement and courage when people chat in the cafes about getting involved or starting a social innovation in their community. You feel it when people smile about hearing other communities who make progress in a positive and meaningful way. You become it when you join a group and participate in a meaningful way – a path to self-actualization and greater contentment. This is where leaders and managers need to exert their desires for real progress, by bringing people together through value systems and by becoming the change we truly wish to see.

Within this book exists research on various authors and disciplines in order to bring a comprehensive and full spectrum approach to managing for social responsibility. There is a lot of work from the fields of organizational development, management science and behaviour to Jungian psychology, team dynamics, philosophy and eco-psychology, as well as practical steps and guidance for implementing new projects or enhancing an existing programme. You will find academic and practical approaches sourced from a mix of journals, books, and the internet. As much as this book is highly referenced, there is much more that could be done to create a case for corporate social responsibility (CSR) and business evolution. There is enough here to alter managers perspectives without having to wait for an economic, societal or environmental crisis, although these are already happening. Without change things will get worse.

If we define our approach to sustainability as the degree of harmony with our natural surroundings, then we have to include more than just technical fixes to our methods of harmful impacts. Making bandages from the same mindset that created the discord with nature in the first place will continue to lead to cumulative and complex impacts such as we are seeing in our economy, society and degradation of the biosphere right now.

Sustainability must include a human fix, a move towards adaptability and acceptance of our destructive nature and a renewal of ethics that sustain relationships amongst each other and this world. This is why I believe old cultures had a cosmic perspective - it allowed them to realize their place in the universe and thus our pace here on earth. We are truly astronauts, visitors here for a while - perhaps unwelcome were we able to read the signs of violence and social injustice that plague our civilization. But not all is wrong. Our mainstream messages may serve to confuse and deliver views of an alien and fantasy lifestyle, especially to our youth, but we are waking to a new time that will create health and well being as the preeminent tools for governance. We must strive to reduce the separation of business from our communities and environment. Using an initiative such as CSR will enable a systems approach to developing a sustainable business model.

This book is written to provide inertia for a new form of management that encompasses the well being of the organization, a more humanistic approach requiring intelligence gathering and an appreciation of values and cultural strengths. This is for people who work with people and want to understand how to run an organization and provide leadership while embracing sustainability. This is not meant to dismiss traditional management practices but to enhance and bring options to managers for meeting the challenges of an insecure future. CSR addresses the void of responsibility that business has historically left to government and communities and is an excellent platform for building a sustainable foundation for future success. I push past the traditional CSR definition and go beyond to bring culture, community and the human psyche to the forefront as valuable assets to assist in making progress for both the business organization and the planet.

ACKNOWLEDGEMENTS

I would like to thank a few people, interesting, intelligent and courageous friends, mentors and souls who have supported me in life and have touched me if even for a moment by kind words or timely advice.

It does not take much, just the right timing, the right communication and an open mind to receive – the same elements I stress so vital for managing organizations for the future.

I extend my gratitude to Tina Rogers for being a stalwart editor, companion and a great example of a person to depend on. Kingsley Dennis for responding to my posts and for doing your own work – please do not stop, we need warriors for good causes. Roy Ehlermann for coffee talks, never underestimate the value of time to just have coffee chat around issues of people and environment. Kenneth Clarke for your support and love of bicycle communities. Robert Bissett for your patience, consulting and co-production of the CSR gaming simulation product. Professors Irene Henriques, Peter Victor, Joe Sheridan, and José Etcheverry for your teaching, guidance and advice. Robert Rogers for giving me a book so many years ago that shifted my thinking and strengthened my belief in kismet and humanity – great timing. Chander Khanna for your patience and our chats about human nature while driving to and fro the noetic sciences meetings. Marc Piccinato because sometimes we all need a friend with which to imbibe and be in the now. Wayne Dyer, for your excellent delivery and sage advice and love for your work. Finally, great and admired influences in life and work from Jon Anderson, Rachel Carson, Deepak Chopra, Wade Davis, Willis Harman, Jane Jacobs, Carl Jung, John Lennon and Joni Mitchell. Peace.

Introduction

Economy, commerce and trade externalize much of the activities of industrial production into societal and natural processes. The market uses rational individual interests to determine the 'best interest' of the society by offering choice through competitiveness. But our choices are not relevant to progress if misinformed. The trumping of consumerism over citizen values demotes camaraderie, stresses competitiveness over cooperation, and promotes conquest as a way to win in the global market, at least that is what we are sold. And what does it mean to win? The impacts reveal themselves as health issues, inequality and species decline. However, science, society and now business itself have proven we can save money, create wealth and improve our processes to healthier standards by working together to conserve nature, but it requires innovation and leadership to take responsibility and political will to bring the necessary change within a tenaciously resistant and reckless global business sector.

The schizophrenic lifestyle people have adopted in westernized cultures sees them account for their family's own health and the wellbeing of their communities, but at work, often values change or no longer have merit within the organization. No longer do nurturing behaviours exhibit themselves, instead, we see subversion to what has been proposed by some as a psychopathic culture (a lack of empathy). Psychopathy is rampant in North America. How much of a cognitive dissonance is it to sacrifice your home, the earth, for profit generation and how does that impact the psyche? We often find ways of distracting ourselves or make excuses for avoiding our responsibility. Our personality disorder is characterized by a disregard for, or violation of, the rights of others, or as anti-social behaviour and the inability to express basic love and compassion in everything we do. It is hard to recognize the corporation, our business organizations, as 'persons' or entities with equivalent rights when they exhibit communal psychopathic behaviour.

This desensitization is responsible for much of the pollution, violence and apathy plaguing the human race. In a large sense, social responsibility is about recognizing our cognitive dissonance or 'split' from our responsibilities as stewards and as human beings to our fellow human. We need to re-empower ourselves within our communities and create stronger ties with our organizations. Intrinsic in caring for each other is caring for the systems of life that support and nurture each other's quality of life. Indeed, a return to traditional community values within the business organization could help alleviate stress, pollution and disease even provide full employment provided organizations plan to accommodate their communities. If our cities be built on the market, then business and renewed ethics could reshape the urban landscape with greener buildings, gardens, better commuting and fair labour practices, chemical reduction, healthy workplace initiatives, and local food options. All of this is and more is possible now, by adopting and going beyond a traditional approach to business and social responsibility and recognizing the power of the people within the organization to bring about this much needed change for our own and our children's future.

What is Corporate Social Responsibility?

There are a number of ways to define social responsibility.

Social responsibility (SR) is an organization's promise to educate itself and engineer new processes to the benefit of shareholders, stakeholders and ecological integrity. There are many definitions to corporate social responsibility. Let's take a look at a few of these and find the common denominator:

UK government defines CSR as the voluntary actions that business can take, over and above compliance with minimum legal requirements, to address both its own competitive interests and the interests of wider society.

The European Commission defines it as a concept whereby companies integrate social and environmental concerns in their business operations and in their stakeholders on a voluntary basis

Another example is the Chinese Ministry of Commerce, the definition being; a concrete action taken by Chinese companies to implement the political aspiration of the new Communist Party collective leadership – putting people first to create a harmonious society.

Also, the Confederation of British Industry defines CSR as the acknowledgement by companies that CSR becomes the perfect tool to begin a cultural change for innovation. It requires systems thinking and an appreciation of community, health, prosperity and relationships. Going beyond philanthropy, it is about empowering workers and co-communities, leveraging competencies and sharing ideas. When handled in an organized and purposeful manner, CSR can be the springboard for a renewal of working spirit and innovation (Crane, Matten, & Spence, 2008).

The above definitions are however passive rather than proactive in their disposition. This book aims to bring a concrete approach to implementation and direction, also allowing for cultural shifts that bring more innovative approaches to mutual benefit of business and planet.

All of these definitions recognize the core characteristics of CSR. The first and prominent notion is that a CSR program is voluntary, but so is innovation. Also, there is recognition of both the positive and negative effects of economic behaviour. Traditionally, impact costs have been deferred to society and environment in terms of health and degradation. CSR requires the acknowledgement and internalizing of these externalities. It is a collaborative approach, gathering input from multiple stakeholders to assist in aligning social and economic goals. It is more than philanthropy. It is organizational development that impacts culture, life-work balance, values, and business practice.

A true CSR program creates improvements to the environmental and resource management in community and organizational enterprise. Some of the obvious benefits are:

- Lower operating costs and resource use
- Attract and retain talented people
- Improved employee performance and commitment
- Customer loyalty based on distinctive ethical values

4

- Stronger corporate risk management strategies
- Enhanced economic and brand value
- Greater revenue streams derived from ethically sources and fair trade products and investments

The initial costs for a CSR program range depending on the depth and breadth of the program. In the case of resource conservation, costs are recouped by savings in materials and energy use. But like any investment there is money, time and human power required. For more social endeavours, costs are converted to the equivalent of public relations and reputation dollars, widened customer base or through innovative partnerships, creating more opportunities. Making a business case will properly lay out the social and environmental costs and benefits for sustainable business practice.

With any opportunity to positively affect a culture, there is potential for a deeper and more meaningful CSR program that goes beyond the tangible – or measurable - benefits. An organization, or any community for that matter, can find, once organized, new methods for counselling each other, greater participation in decision making, increased innovation and resilience, and more meaningful relationships. All of these higher order attributes are a measure of an organization's greatest asset – knowledge.

We become what we learn. Knowledge management forms the basis of institutional legacy. The history, traditions, and lessons learned from years of practice are invaluable in bringing others into the culture of an organization and maintaining intellectual capital. Insight and experiences can be captured and shared in a number of ways, and exist in both implicit and explicit forms. Implicit or tacit knowledge is the wisdom of the work, things that cannot be instantly performed but are taught and practised. Explicit knowledge is factual, archived and exists in an accessible form - like data or media. Sharing ways of knowing will be important in topics in the roles of leadership, governance and in partnering with other organizations and communities.

CSR can help relieve organizational dysfunction by addressing core cultural and process issues. You may recognize that your workplace is a creature of habit, predictably reacting to business issues in the same fashion over and over, perhaps using outdated behaviours or frustrating managers and co-workers. An organization's myopic approach is evident when current circumstances are viewed as previous ones have been and thus are addressed with the same routines used in the past. Perhaps the knowledge management system is closed to new techniques or ideas, and this is leading to increased stagnation and lack of creativity. Leaders must signal that times have changed, discourage dysfunctional behaviour and reinforce new workflows that reflect the reality of the situation and open the mind.

There is also a social innovation component that remains ambiguous and whose benefits are often overlooked. Organizations may not realize the full potential of undertaking a CSR unless a cultural change is desired from the bottom up. Rarely do workers take responsibility to initiate a cultural change they believe in for the welfare of the organization. Either management discourages big thinkers or is dedicated to an outmoded command and conquer model. Because CSR is linked to our intrinsic values, it can be a tool for increasing the intangible wealth of the organization. Intangible assets include knowledge, talent, awareness, innovation, creativity and influence. With a proper approach, a CSR program has the potential to bring out the best in people and unleash their individual and team potential.

What is a 21st century organization?

Corporations, communities, institutions are all forms of human organization structured for a purpose. They are networks of people to facilitate a unified end-goal. By working together, people achieve more than working apart. In a good organization, we develop personal mastery with the support of others and are encouraged and mentored by those wiser than us. In the best case, we learn more about how we function as individuals in group settings and about how the world really works and how our organization fits into the grand scheme of things. In its most basic form, an organization has a leader, managers and workers and a singular purpose. It requires resources, information and a desire for progress or a goal that sees a change of state in its present for to a desired future state. The best forms of organization are efficient, productive, creative, fair, intelligent and flexible. With the inclusion of CSR, the best organizations are also socially and environmentally responsible.

Want to diminish an organization's worth? Employ a leader who does not recognize the abilities of others to contribute to the greater cause. Everyone knows a type of manager and dreads ever needing to spend time with this inept or negative individual. These people create misery, are individualistic, parasitic, and infest their subordinates with a creeping cynicism reducing the efficacy of the team. They put their team-mates in positions that they themselves would never assume and fail to see opportunities or issues even when proposed to them directly. Some organizations are so bulky and bureaucratic that these slothful and ornery individuals persist like bedbugs. As long as the routine routinely runs, then so shall this individual. This is where a mission and values statement falls upon deaf ears. There is no chance here that an organization fostering bad management stands for something more than selfish profitability, simple market share, or stock performance and that anyone working there truly believes it would be worth saving should tough times occur. Under these circumstances, individuals find themselves working under obligation status. Talented individuals leave and the business will eventually degrade as the Enrons, Lehman Brothers, and WorldComs of the business world show.

An organization that fosters a positive learning environment will be fertile ground for good change. Members are emotionally committed to making great things happen and will faithfully execute the required tasks with creativity and enthusiasm. With an open-minded environment, people can bring their concerns for the organization into a global context and freely discuss the extent of the problems facing the organization, including those faced by the global economy, society and planet. They acknowledge the seriousness of the financial, social and environmental difficulties and take responsibility for their duties and share of the problems. This is the future of organization – dynamic, flexible, intelligent and virtuous.

The Challenges

Earth's population reached seven billion people by the end of the year 2010. All of these people requiring energy, space and a network of relationships to co-exist on this world were born into a dichotomy of values. In the western world or the northern hemisphere (depending which map you use), talk of abundance and attracting all the wealth you want, on the eastern or southern side, talk of raising their standard of living and bringing good food and clean water to everyone. With our present mode of productivity and economy, neither is possible but we persist and insist that we deserve all our modern conveniences without making the big changes we really need to see. All of this assumes we need to sacrifice our own quality of life in order to be more socially just and environmentally friendly, and that is a fallacy.

The singular perspective of profit driving is missing most of what being truly productive is all about. We believe better life is equated with more money. But when it's quality of life we're after and we have a good understanding of what that means, we have the power to create wealth and health at the same time. Considering money only represents resources, it to is limited by the planet's capacity to produce. Existing for profit only is an ethically hollow stance and a dangerous one to the wellbeing of the planet. Besides the inequality in profit-sharing and the social injustice that our waste produces, succumbing to the profit-only dogma imbues a carelessness and reckless abandon towards society and environment. I believe business could do better if they take a new approach. What if it could border on heroic? What if there was an industrial revolution created by business itself that led the way to a fair and healthy society in which we all contribute to wellbeing and development?

To become a force for positive change, an organization must embrace a community culture that includes life and health and the pursuit of happiness, not just for the few, but for the many employees and stakeholders involved. Profit can be measured in many ways, it's possible to attract and retain the best and most talented people based on values and not just salary. Business will have to undergo a core cultural change to free up the intangible resources and energy that

8

comes from commitment, rather than mere compliance. In a dynamic and connected world, new networks must be able to form ad hoc between business and social communities and knowledge must flow freely and openly to discuss business and environmental matters and opportunities in the same breath with no fear of repercussions to the worker or team member.

And what of sharing information? How is it that social media creates greater awareness of social and environmental conditions and how can it change the way we do business?

Because patronage decisions are being made independently of mainstream advertising, there is a shift to purchase and do business with those who recognize our own personal values. These values can be found inside the various virtual and real communities of the world. Social media has had a significant impact in the way we network for information and create relationships. But what now of the effects of the social information age on organizations and the way they conduct their activities? Most can agree that unless a business meets its legal and ethical obligations to society it should go extinct. Corporate responsibility is one way in which an organization can begin to adopt practices, knowledge and behaviour that will eventually lead them down a path to be part of the new economy and be included in the good ranks of public perception through integrity, not deception. All of this is bringing corporate culture to the cusp of an ethical, humanistic and higher purpose for society and the planet.

The new leadership will assume responsibility and adapt to the changes for the organization's sake, understanding social and environmental impacts and share in creating the people's vision. In a rush to be productive we leave behind our ability to contemplate our direction. Corporations, institutions and communities need to be able forecast the pressures of globalization, resource scarcity, hyper-competition, technology, and social change just to maintain a quality of life. A failure to recognize limits and constraints will bring an unfortunate demise.

Quality of life at work and home will be redefined, with less emphasis on materialism and structure and more on service, flexibility and ingenuity. How people modify their behaviour will be a result of shared foresight, leadership and collaborative effort towards the common good. Now we can see how corporate social responsibility is a response to the growing social and environmental pressures. CSR reporting is now mainstream with nearly 80% of the 250 largest firms on the planet issuing reports (Shuili, Bhattacharya, & Sankar). However, if applied with the same thinking that has reduced planning effectiveness, CSR will be a bandage where we need preventative and proactive measures.

This book examines our current thinking dilemma in the context of organizational change and the need for planning sustainable development – a new beginning. In this book, I redefine and address sustainable development and what it means to organizational structure and behaviour. I apply the principles of a corporate social responsibility approach but go beyond that by including the importance of knowledge management, innovation, cultural and behavioural considerations, and even psychology, all of which needs to be part of the DNA of an organizational strategy before a truly responsible organization can function in the new economy.

We Need A New Planning Approach

Organizations can cope and succeed in volatile environments by employing three tools: 1) stakeholder engagement, 2) proactive learning and; 3) a new planning approach.

These tools require a shift in thinking and a cultural change that reflects the need for business to become part of the solution to making progress on economic, social and environmental challenges that affect us all. The 'for-profit' and 'not-for-profit' agencies will merge in to a 'for benefit' corporation in which profit and social benefit are the balanced mainstay of the firm. We see this happening now with so many NGO partnerships today.

Progress and productivity are no longer strategized around human resources but around resource based economies. The science and technology managing our resources is now dictating future policy as we become efficient and effective knowledge workers around resource use. By constantly scanning our environment, we gather information and make decisions to set new policy direction. The intelligence we apply to creating a new function or activity reflects the depth and breadth of information we gather. By combining technique derived from enhanced learning with increasing capacity for gathering information, we reach the pinnacle of decision making based on the state of economy, society and environment. Anything else would be a constricted and compartmentalized view of reality. Now add a motivated network of people to assist in co-creating a solution and we have an organization ready for meeting future challenges.

However, there needs to be a fundamental shift in organizational structure to affect culture. Most organizations are structured for quantity not quality and are losing talent and productivity because of the lack of values alignment in the organizations to the various stakeholder communities. The implicit moral underpinning required for eliminating the harm of business impacts and increasing the social benefit of business activity has for the most part evaporated, losing legitimacy and risking their social licence to operate.

There is an epidemic of apathy and lethargy towards work in the workplace. Employees revealed in a Gallup Poll of almost 25 million people, that they are disengaged from their jobs (Ehin, 2009). This is a waste of time, energy and human potential and is a direct result of how the organization is structured and led. Thus the need to address corporate culture in developing a holistic CSR strategy.

Leadership and management must be the company's oracle, looking into the future and seeing the possibilities, engaging people on a personal level for motivation and to carry a mission that includes a higher purpose. Globalization has altered strategy, but sometimes the goals of expansion don't reflect the reality of the approaches needed to be a part of the future. Professors of business Gary Hamel and C. K. Prahalad's research has confirmed that top managers spend only 3 per cent of their time actually thinking about the future, the rest of the time is acting in response (Hamel & Prahalad, 1994). This explains

11

why critical trends and paths can be completely overlooked and opportunities missed.

A truly effective Corporate Responsibility strategy is designed to create a substantial cultural shift and a new awareness in the approach to planning. The problem with current CSR practice is that the common corporate response has been neither strategic nor operational but cosmetic (Porter & Kramer, 2006) and I would argue incremental rather than strategic. Thus, a strategy that integrates CSR into the core business functions and culture will unleash the creative potential of employees and bring new business. Research suggests 87% of Americans would switch brands, price and quality being equal, if one brand is associated with a good cause (Shuili et al.).

The key to obtaining a social licence to operate is by addressing the real social and environmental issues on a local level. Avoiding responsibility will cost more in the long run. For example, China, in its zeal to become a premier economic power and material provider to the world is reported to have costs of up to $36 billion in lost industrial output just due to water shortages, $13 billion in acid rain, $6 billion in desertification and urbanization, and the list goes on (Elizabeth Economy and Kenneth Lieberthal, HBR). These cost are accumulating natural interest in more than just dollars each and every day. There will be skyrocketing health costs and collapse of natural systems that provide food, clean water and valuable natural resources. Climate change is poised to create havoc with weather and the economy. The Stern Review, commissioned by the Chancellor of the Exchequer and reporting to the British Prime Minister, assessed the economic impacts of climate change. The conclusions are a call to action. The report calls climate change "…the greatest and widest-ranging market failure ever seen." (OCC, 2006). Basically, climate change can bring the economy to a halt if action is taken later rather than sooner; the business-as-usual (BAU) scenario.

0°C	1°C	2°C	3°C	4°C	5°C

Food

Falling crop yields in many developing regions

Severe impacts in marginal Sahel region

Rising number of people at risk from hunger (25 – 60% increase in the 2080s in one study with weak carbon fertilisation), with half of the increase in Africa and West Asia.

Entire regions experience major declines in crop yields (e.g. up to one third in Africa)

Rising crop yields in high-latitude developed countries if strong carbon fertilisation

Yields in many developed regions decline even if strong carbon fertilisation

Water

Small mountain glaciers disappear worldwide – potential threat to water supplies in several areas

Significant changes in water availability (one study projects more than a billion people suffer water shortages in the 2080s, many in Africa, while a similar number gain water

Greater than 30% decrease in runoff in Mediterranean and Southern Africa

Sea level rise threatens major world cities, including London, Shanghai, New York, Tokyo and Hong Kong

Ecosystems

Coral reef ecosystems extensively and eventually irreversibly damaged

Possible onset of collapse of part or all of Amazonian rainforest

Large fraction of ecosystems unable to maintain current form

Many species face extinction (20 – 50% in one study)

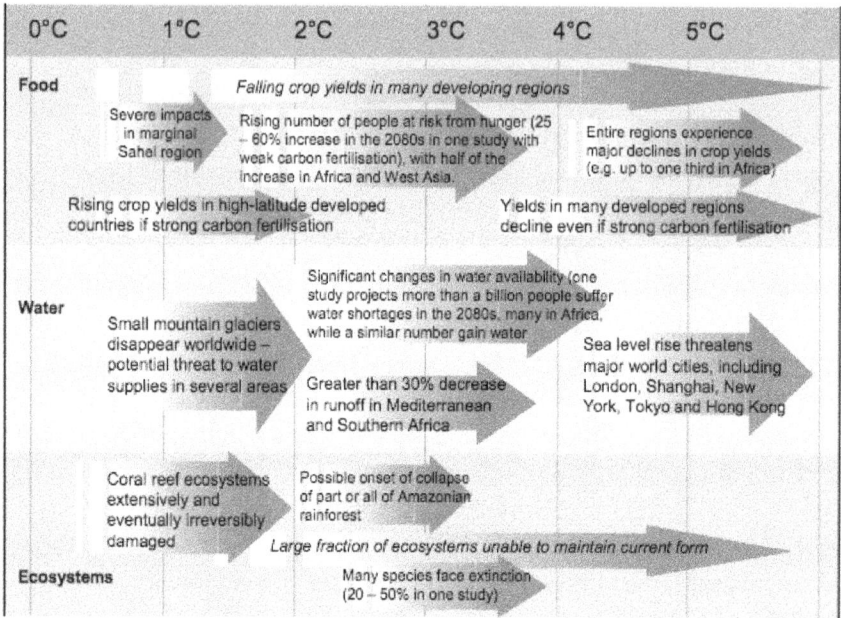

Climate change and environmental concerns can be addressed within a CSR program. As companies look to do their part, ride-share programs, alternative travel arrangements, green supply chains, teleworking, net meetings, and energy efficiency programs have all become popular among CEOs, cost cutters and employees. The success of such programs is directly dependent on a shift in organizational behaviour and process. "The removal of barriers to behavioural change is a third essential element, one that is particularly important in encouraging the take-up of opportunities for energy efficiency"(OCC, 2006, p. 20). The Stern Review continues in suggesting needed changes and highlighting potential barriers that include a lack of reliable information, transaction costs, and behavioural and organizational inertia. One such failure is the lack of business foresight to adopt cost-effective energy efficiency strategies that represents a lack of competency, incomplete planning or managerial desire.

The compass of corporate direction must represent the values of people within the business to deliver a product or service that reflects the human and natural systems of which we are all a part, thereby reflecting societal values or even influencing them. Although CSR has been around for over 40 years, greater awareness now makes CSR an essential tool for sustainable and strategic business success. By also addressing the social and environmental components, CSR can help merge the goals of the individual with the goals of the organization and to the broader realm of stakeholders. Consumers become more than just purchasers, they become champions for a cause.

CSR can sometimes be equated with philanthropy. Donating to local charities has the advantage of using local knowledge to distribute the social investment, however, many charities lack the competencies to deliver the social outcomes beyond the period of investment, creating a resources dependence instead of independence, the aim of sustainability (Nwankwo, Phillips, & Tracey, 2007). With a strategic CSR program, community enterprise becomes an option, thus building capacity in the partnering organization and a mutually beneficial relationship with the community.

CSR is business's way of evolving to meet global challenges associated with sustainability. It should not be about reacting to regulations or suppliers facing resource scarcity, rather it should be a multi-dimensional approach involving economic, social and environmental concerns. Institutions and communities are also coming to terms with defining sustainable development, the core ethic of which stems from the familiar Brundtland definition, "...the ability to meet the needs of the present without compromising the future" (Brundtland & World Commission on Environment and Development., 1987). However, to be fair, the activity of CSR continues to carry debate. Business decisions continue to be made distinct from ethical ones by separating the business out from society. This view sees CSR as something that should not be the organization's mandate as it takes resources away from the firm's principal function. This dualism fades when individuals and groups are viewed as a part of the larger systems of society and its institutions and thus business must be involved in co-creating progress for sustainability.

This book was written to assist in creating the understanding that is needed on the organizational level, community and business working together, to shift our thinking and practices so we can manage our negative impacts better and be ready for the changes to come. It includes planning theory and practice, organizational development and behaviour, sociology, psychology and common sense. It also includes a clarion call to leaders to hear your hearts and employ compassion in business practice. Many of the practices and ideas within this book are applicable to community engagement and business improvement as well as team and personal growth.

Engaging in corporate social responsibility requires a long-term commitment and investment, but the rewards of creating shared value can go beyond anything that revenue could possibly buy. An organization can reduce their footprint in environmental damage, or create a supply-chain free from labour issues, lower cancer rates by reducing chemical involvement, reduce emissions, any change of which affects our communities over time. Through a process of stakeholder buy-in, a firm can build long-term relationships and assets with a good CSR program. It is in the understanding that we exist in a socially constructed world that business will be the champion for future prosperity and not its destructor.

Finally, CSR can also be a core mission for public institutions and communities. When all the barriers are taken away and we are stripped of all our labels and roles, we are all people with the same needs for health, respect and accomplishment. At the end of sustainability's rainbow, the ethical corporation will be the only one with the moral authority to lead.

By yourself, you may travel faster, together, we will travel farther. – African proverb

Perspectives on Sustainable Development

Corporate Social Responsibility, Corporate Social Responsiveness or Corporate Social Performance, whichever term you choose, are all related to reducing human impacts on the environment and improving social relations. Terms aside, it really is a sustainability planning program for the organization, and demands that the corporation's
15

development is one that operates as an open system that takes in resources, human and environmental, and emits outputs. This includes interaction with legal, political and natural environments.

We often think and visualize sustainability as a balanced approach to planning and practice in the areas of economic, social and environmental activity. This is like comparing apples and oranges and can be misleading in determining progress. If we look at sustainability as a collection of systems, we look beyond cause and effect to interrelationships and cycles of processes with other systems.

The following graphic depicts three Venn diagrams showing our current perspectives surrounding sustainability.

> The *Traditional* view is that human activity takes a balanced approach that incorporates consideration of the three aspects of economy, society and environment. This view, although an improvement over no view, is a naïve approach to sustainable development. The perception of structure affects our way of thinking and as a result, shapes our planning and delivery of solutions.
>
> The *Logical* approach is one that more accurately depicts how systems are nested within each other. All humans are nested with the cycling systems of the environment. The economy is a human construct of society and not all people practice market economy. Now we have a more accurate perspective of the systems we interact with and how we can approach problem solving.
> The third view, which I propose as being the most accurate view, is the *Practical* view of sustainability.

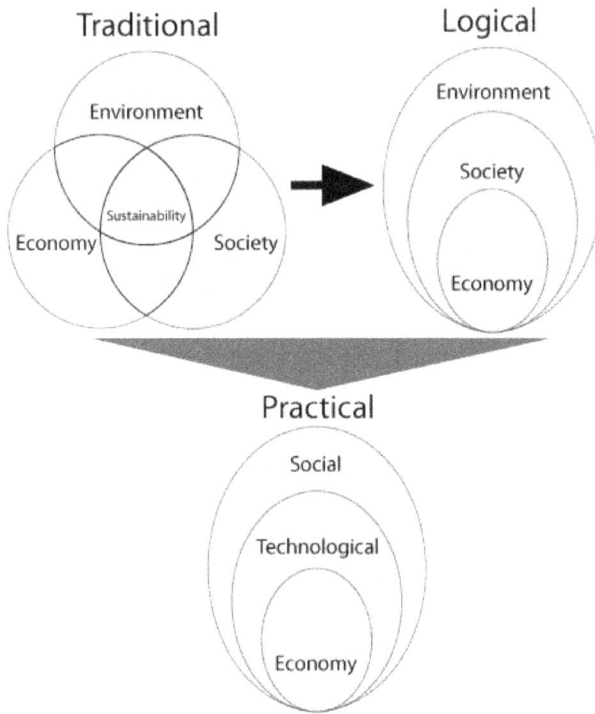

Traditional

Environment

Economy Sustainability Society

Logical

Environment

Society

Economy

Practical

Social

Technological

Economy

The Practical view of sustainable development is constructed with economy nested within a technological sphere and both completely nested with the social sphere. The reasons for this are:

The term 'environmental management' is, from a planetary perspective, an oxymoron. The environment manages us. We never have been able to manage the environment, although our desire to tame and control nature is expressed in our urbanization through paving over watersheds, damming rivers and releasing harmful waste into our air and oceans. We can only really manage ourselves and our activities and impacts. Thus, all problem solving is a social issue related to our knowledge, awareness and behaviour and must be derived from that. Technology has become so pervasive as to become a social medium and the largest influence on the economy. If we are to approach sustainable development, we need to apply technology to assist us in creating the skills (new techniques) and allow us to craft solutions to re-invent ourselves, without being a detriment to the planet. We also need to be savvy of the problems of technology

17

adoption with respect to social interactions, dependency and competition.

The economy must be addressed as an artefact of social and technological fusion. The economy does no harm. Humans do harm through the impacts of creating certain types of perceived value to society. I stress 'certain' because not all value generation is necessarily good. While a material item may create trade and value, the processing and disposal of that item may have long-term impacts that far outweigh any value the trade has produced, to both the supplier and consumer. As I alluded to before, social and environmental costs are externalized by trading within the market economy, but this is changing.

Any organization with a growth mandate needs to account for more than the logistics and capital budget models required for expansion and should include accounting for social and environmental factors. In meeting these obligations, the organizational planner has the technical challenges of finding water, waste sinks, carbon sinks, food security, green infrastructure, chemical reductions and policy revision to encourage sustainable development (Bugliarello, 2006, p. 21).

Prevention is better than a cure. If we do not correctly recognize signs and symptoms of illness in our systems, we cannot hope to recognize interpretations that we create as a way to communicate and share these illnesses. For example, a recent decline in bees has meant billions of dollars of lost food from lack of pollination, but what of the causes and cumulative impacts of bee decline to other systems, social and environmental? What linkages should we be actually looking at that will tell us what forces that system is being affected by and affecting? When Albert Einstein stated that we would have four years to live if all the bees disappeared, he was remarking on our intimate connections with other living systems. As a physicist, he could see how energy and matter interacted and how behaviour in one species impacts another. Managers act like a physicist when they perform activities to economize and maximize energy and resource use and also as ecologists by acting in ways that protect the commons and secure the larger welfare (Wood, 2010).

Sustainability from a human perspective is a social ethic that is developed through combined expression, knowledge and action, the expression resulting in the institutionalization of the ethic in our culture. There is no sense in achieving partial sustainability. That would simply be buying time rather than shifting the mindset or belief system that does harm in the first place.

Because sustainability is an expression in connectedness, networks must form that allow knowledge transfer to induce a positive change in group or community behaviour. That's part one. Part two to sustainability would be how the network manages and directs resources; the processes of the system or the economics involved. Thus, it is a combination of network, knowledge and organizational behaviour. The organization, whether corporate or community needs to build bridges of networks, share knowledge and apply the resulting innovation to the structure and flow of resources through the organization to achieve sustainable results.

I repeat, we cannot stop at simply *reducing* unsustainability. We all consume resources within depleting and renewing cycles of the planet. It's the way we consume and the resulting waste product that makes us so inefficient and destructive to the natural processes we rely upon. Any halfway attempt is a call for a renewed ethic to guide our behaviour, which means cultural change. This change is happening in rural areas and on the streets of cities, but will institutions and businesses be able to match those new values?

With so many companies structured as an inflexible hierarchy, the owners and leaders are almost solely held accountable. Business ethics are now at the forefront of news stories and economic recovery criticism. To strike an analogy, just as the 'Hummer' vehicle has disappeared, so too will the wasteful, bloated and narcissistic CEO. Ford motors has struck gold by not accepting bailout money and reinvented its image with an ethical stance that has become so attractive to buyers, that they have had the most successful increase in sales for years. The new corporate ethical stance is compact, efficient and smart. The new corporate culture is strategic, compassionate and wise.

19

CSR necessitates a long-term perspective and strategy to resource planning. Sustainability is about saving the future and considering others in our actions and behaviours. It is time for assuming responsibility for our actions, hold others accountable for theirs, and understand that working collaboratively will be the only way to overcome the differences in views, cultures and resources. But something is quickly becoming a precious commodity, more than money: time. With time becoming a scarce resource, we risk becoming trapped in the kind of short-term thinking that is at the root of the problems we are experiencing today. We are focussed on narrow fixed points, paying attention to single events and their particular causes.

Based on the premise that sustainability is about balancing economic, social and environmental priorities, the balance may be hard to achieve. "To cultures more drawn to novelty, growth, discovery, and conquest, the pursuit of balance may never generate broad enthusiasm or become a galvanizing goal." (Mulvihill & Milan, 2007, pp. 658-659). Social institutions reinforce particular views of the world, applying "…their own standards to the puzzles and problems on which they work…though two paradigms may seem to apply the same concepts, they mean quite different things by them. Both imply that people who work within different paradigms see the world and any problems that they face quite differently." (Pidd, 2004, p. 18).

Clearly, we are attempting to solve the world's problems with the same type of thinking that created them. This also implies that systems now in use are constructed on the economic paradigm of old.

John Ehrenfeld, a leader in the emerging field of industrial ecology, asks that we take a hard look at ourselves and examine our own behaviours, assumptions, personal satisfaction, and technology. John questions the mainstream definition of sustainability and gets to the point of proposing a pragmatic perspective that should guide a framework for personal, social, and economic decision-making. John outlines the way to build a real business case for sustainability. Rather than shifting the burden and focusing on the symptoms as many companies do, Ehrenfeld attacks the roots.

If one accepts the strictly economic functional view of an organization, then making progress in sustainability has to reflect the relationship between CSR and financial performance to influence business behaviour. However, this ignores any duty bound to managers to be accountable for the impacts of business operations. Sustainable development, as it is now, is defined by its unsustainable nature. We can manage 'unsustainability', quantify the world around us and measure our consumption, but how about managing something as aspirational as sustainability or industrial ecology? This requires new modes of thinking and perceiving.

Tom Galdwin, University of Michigan Professor, has classified some 20 unsustainable characteristics that underlie social and individual activities in today's society (Ehrenfeld, 2004, p. 6):

Cognitive	Worldview	Contemporary Norms	Psychological
Reductionist	Atomistic	Efficiency	Repression
Proximity	Mechanistic	Quantitative	Denial
Simplicity	Anthropocentric	Secularism	Projection
Certainty	Rationalistic	Narcissism	Rationalization
Discrepancy	Individualistic	Techno-optimism	Insulation

We can see how these characteristics could influence our daily lives in a negative way, yet we continue to socially manufacture them in the workplace. We can also draw direct impacts on the effectiveness and efficiency of an organization with these characteristics in mind. The whole of the culture of the organization is unwittingly driven by the wrong characteristics, some of which are recognizable within this table.

The tendency to be individualistic also affects the organizations of which we are a part. Reward structures in organizations favour the individual and perpetuate certain types of behaviour not conducive to internal network building, and good relationship forming. It is becoming a rarity that individuals have the commitment to their community of co-workers and partners that goes beyond the basic job descriptions.

Reliance on Technology - The Undermining of Technique

Technology is the dominant business tool today. The notion of competitiveness demands that constant upgrading and reinforcing of information systems to process more, faster. Our personal lives are moving the same way. We, as individuals, attempt to retain relevance within the economic system and so we make personal investment into upgrading ourselves and acquiring technology in the home, taking precious time out of our own lives to invest in learning corporate products. It is so pervasive that personal devices are a must. We now process so much information through technology that it has come to dominate our social behaviours and communications. We keep our skills and even our memories in devices, no longer having to rely on our own competencies. How many times have we heard 'there is an app for that!'.

22

We must beware of the reliance on technology in re-organizing ourselves. Technology can lend competitive advantage but is also expensive, can be unreliable, creates dependence and may be redundant over time. Technique is another matter. Good organizations realize the quality of people working for them is at the core of meeting organizational objectives. The skills and wisdom we develop over time through experience, change organizations in the same way technology has changed society. But just as the development of technology has been conditioned by political, cultural and economic factors, so have our techniques.

The focus on technology as progress has perpetuated a wave of cultural extinction. In *The Wayfinders: Why Ancient Wisdom Matters in the Modern World*, Wade Davis stresses the importance of preserving not only nature but also cultures that have inspired people to live ecologically sustainable lives for millennia. He shows us the importance of knowing who we are, where we have come from and the ethic of sustaining the world; not trying to improve upon it by treating it as a commodity. As an enthnographer and anthropologist, Wade reminds us we have cultural memory that is being lost, a warning shared by Jane Jacobs in her book *Dark Age Ahead*. Both authors agree that the lack of traditional knowledge transfer and skills will create civilizational upheaval – a dark age.

"We have created a reliance on the extraordinary capabilities of modern technology for everything from city building to military security, from pollution controls to treating disease. However, all of these issues have a social component, which must be addressed. Implementing a technical fix without involving the social and cultural measures will lead to ultimate failure." (Pacey, 1994).

Reliance on technology can lead to self-justification for continuing obsolete processes. Arnold Pacey inquires as to how we view and evaluate progress. One example he cites is food production. By focusing on production as the only indicator, we may see a graph trend upward, leading us to a belief that current processes are performing well. This one-dimensional view can lead to less desirable development elsewhere. In Britain, food production has increased enormously in the last century, especially in relation to the area of land used and the number of people employed. But output per unit of energy consumed on farms has decreased (ibid, p. 14). Taking a narrow perspective on progress creates a narrow belief system, which then alters or reinforces behaviours according to that belief.

During the electrical blackout that crippled seven north-eastern states in the USA and southern Ontario in 2003, people lined up at gas stations reliant on credit and debit cards that were not accepted, their automobiles and anything that required electricity was now valueless.

Productivity ground to a halt. As people headed out to the streets, they noticed the night sky for the first time, void of light pollution, and people exclaimed about how 'quiet' everything was. No hum of machinery and electricity or cars grinding by as rubber kisses the asphalt. Just a sense of peace as there was nothing to distract us from coming together to chat about what was happening. It was a social miracle - and a potential disaster had people not self-organized and cooked the food in their fridge for sharing with others in the community.

The use of technology must be differentiated from the programs driving technology. The network structure and technology infrastructure is just as applicable to developing a sustainable economy as it is to facilitating private profits. The only difference is the way information is processed and the transparency of the functions that alter that information. Like an electronic gambling machine computing to ensure the odds remain astronomical or a gas pump that may skip a cent for every dollar pumped, technology is bent to the will of its masters and can be architected with an ethic to either help or take advantage of systems just like anything else. This may explain the rise of open source programming as an alternative to private operating systems. The use of restricted information and structured input and output mechanisms can only be part of an organization equation for progress just because of the loss of real world data.

As we come to rely on technology more to facilitate communications, we also come to reduce the context of our messaging and our habits for providing context-rich information. Over time we lose general context with cultural norms of behaviour, and adopt a way of being that facilitates technology. The debate on the role of technology in society has yet to fully take place. When so much technology is geared toward a disposable economy, how much is put toward a sustainable society? Greenpeace reports that e-waste makes up over five per cent of all municipal solid waste and Asia discards an estimated 12 million tonnes a year. Was the productivity or the progression associated with all that waste worth the energy, production, use, and discard of the manufactured product?

- The average lifespan of computers in developed countries has dropped from six years in 1997 to two years in 2005.
- Mobile phones have a lifecycle of less than two years in developed countries.
- 183 million computers were sold worldwide in 2004 - 11.6 per cent more than in 2003.
- 674 million mobile phones were sold worldwide in 2004 - 30 per cent more than in 2003.
- By 2010, there will be 716 million new computers in use. There will be 178 million new computer users in China, 80 million new users in India. (See the Greenpeace website www.greenpeace.org)

The technological communications medium affects trust and norms of social engagement. The difference between meeting and developing a relationship with someone in person as opposed to a chat room poses all sorts of trust and engagement issues. The same goes for organizational processes in developing trust and culture. Technology used as a social medium requires that implicit trust be instated first to properly engage in meaningful exchange. Although technology facilitates virtual teamwork for productivity in organizations, one may decline for instance, lending of money to a virtual team-mate if asked by email. This may even constitute a form of 'spam' perhaps. However, some recent changes in the way technology is programmed and used in communications to create social value explains the boom in social media.

We all have beliefs and values, and values need to be expressed for us to have a self-identity. It is difficult to leave them at the door when entering a social engagement or the workplace and operate independently of a lifetime of beliefs. We feel more at home when we are surrounded by people with similar values and can express deeply our desires to others. The ability to communicate concerns or ideas denotes our integrity, and it is most important that people can relate to those thoughts and feelings in order to form a relationship: a social confirmation.

Whether misery loves company or happy people attract happy people, we manifest and reflect out internal feelings outwardly in hopes that they will be understood. Any form of organization is a psychological experiment with all the dynamics. The disciplines of organizational behaviour and change management are steeped in psychology, social theory and practice.

People and businesses are constantly attempting to express values through social media technology. The processing of information and the ability to make it searchable has created databases of millions of people looking for friends, love, jobs, goods, or just a group to discuss almost anything. The power of this mass collaboration is built on shared values. The internet, in my opinion, is the most untapped resource to create an economic and social revolution that would benefit both trade and community provided it is based on good values and the true value of goods. Democracy and privacy on the internet will become a much larger issue as control of information becomes a tool for regulation as we are already seeing in many countrys.

Healthy relationships are the cornerstones of our lives. Bonnie Montano and Robbie Dillon make some observations in a study that show how technology can be used to strengthen relationships within an organization. The success of technology in creating a group medium is based on membership. Technology enhances connectiveness with a group when it is easy to use, when the same technology is being used and the group is exclusive, facilitating a feeling of membership (Montano & Dillon, 2005).

Many of us use technology on a regular basis but have little or no knowledge and literacy as to how it actually works. We judge a system's use based on convenience, informativeness and relevancy, the combination of which relates to the performance or how much enhancement we gain from engaging with the technology. We have evolved from evaluating character and humanistic values such as compassion, integrity and honour to assessing speed, usefulness and pertinence. Many organizations also assess candidates or group members by the same criteria we judge technology. In this way, we have failed to objectively assess how changes to our culture due to technology have influenced our judgement in communities as well. We need go no further than the political system to see how de-humanized and technocratic the bureaucratic form has become.

The power of information technology becomes apparent when it is combined with a common ethic or value shared by a large group of people. It takes one individual to create and design a web site with enough savvy to develop an interactive forum for communicating an issue and gather feedback for orchestrating a mass demonstration. Economies are created in such ways. Thousands of people come together from virtual space and then into physical space to share their desire for expression and group commitment. Unlike sites such as Facebook, the corporation -with all its investment in technology - fails to come close to rallying this type of support and value creation for its own mission and objectives from its own employees. **The implementation of a CSR program that utilizes technology aimed at unifying people around similar values can unleash that potential if done properly.**

The Use of Technology

- Understand the difference between technology and technique
- Use technology as a tool instead of a dependency
- Know how the technology works to utilize it properly

Conscious Shift to the New Economy

Privatize the Profits, Socialize the Risks. ~ Anonymous

The consumer economy that developed post-war, out of rapid expansion due to fossil fuel technology, has provided much material wealth but the long-term effects of production still remain to be seen. By examining the impacts of the oil fuel technology through a sustainability lens we can broadly agree that the economy has grown, social complexity and problems have grown and environmental degradation has grown. One step forward, two steps back.

One can argue that if all this material wealth has been created then there must be more productivity. Yes and no.

We can claim productivity in the industrial sense of converting resources (earth systems) to consumable products, perhaps. We continue to build bigger more powerful machines to rip up the earth, tear down forests, catch more fish, and get from stoplight to stoplight with ever more frustration. But the primary earth support systems (forests, oceans, flora and fauna) that made these same increases in quality and quantity of living possible are being made less productive, with some systems nearing complete non-productivity.

Harvard University Professor Edward Wilson writes about the tragedy of biodiversity loss on the UNESCO website: "The causes of species extinction are, in order of magnitude of impact on biodiversity, summarized in the acronym HIPPO: Habitat destruction, Invasive species, Pollution, human over-Population, Overharvesting by hunting and fishing. Climate change is definitely a big H." (http://www.unesco.org/new/en/media-services/single-view/news/edward_o_wilson_the_loss_of_biodiversity_is_a_tragedy/back/18384/).

Oceans and fisheries is an example of how we are improperly monitoring our production/consumption processes. We have all enjoyed meals made from seafood or fish, providing beneficial proteins and amino acids that assist our own body systems to

28

maintain health. With respect and understanding of the sacredness of life, we may consume to survive, but the consumer ethic is much different than that. It is tied into our psychological profiles and desire to fulfil the ego, which does not comprehend the need to consider others. It only needs attention for itself.

To highlight my point, the impending collapse of ocean fisheries is well known and well reported:

- Science, November 3 2006, "Impacts of Biodiversity Loss on Ocean Ecosystem Services"
- New York Times, November 3 2006, "Study Sees 'Global Collapse' of Fish Species"
- New Scientist, February 18 2002, "Complete collapse of North Atlantic fishing predicted"

The study posted in Science, revealed that data shows fish catches are 10% below maximum catches with 29% of currently fished species considered collapsed. This is aside from the toxicity we have created within food chains that include these species; this is consumption only. Dolphins now contain enough mercury within them to make us ill (were we to eat them) because of the industrial waste and garbage being dumped into the oceans. Properly managing our consumption means considering all the systems with which we interact, waste and pollution cycles, water quality and quantity, and habitat health for the species we consume. Only then can we truly define productivity, anything else is an illusion. Thus the first step in consciousness raising is awareness and opening up to systems thinking to see that business is a part of the ecology of living systems.

Awareness of ethical business behaviour is playing an increasingly critical role in determining which organizations receive a social licence to operate. It is argued that analysis at the institutional level should reveal if a business has a right to survive. If it cannot be profitable in legal and ethical ways then society has a right to eliminate it. Wood's discretionary principle highlights management's obligation, "Managers are moral actors. Within every domain of corporate social responsibility, they are obliged to exercise such discretion as is available to them, toward socially responsible

29

outcomes (D.J Wood, 1991)". This means managers cannot rightly choose or be forced to perform socially irresponsible acts. Decision making must become a social and not an individual exercise, which means including the client or consumer as a stakeholder (and by extension other species) and administering to individual levels of duty. But ethics vary at the individual level and the manager must be savvy at aligning stakeholders to the vision. Consumers are quick to claim rights but may balk at claiming responsibility.

New Business Ethics

Growing awareness of human impacts on the environment can often highlight inefficiencies in an organisation's activities. No longer is reputation based simply on brand and public relations but on process and the end result or impact on quality of life indicators such as health and education. Globalisation has increased the reach of business but also the network of feedback from the public and awareness of how business operates on social and political levels. This is both a curse and an opportunity to build relationships. For business, integrity must align with strategy and integration must align with society to build a sustainable enterprise.

One problem for sustainable organization building may be in the ethical decision-making process. It begins with the awareness that a moral problem or situation exists. For CSR it is the degrading social and environmental conditions in our communities. By highlighting a moral issue as significant, it is more likely to receive attention and create ethical behaviour. All decisions have an ethical component even though one's sensitivity or skill may not be able to identify the ethics involved.

Making a decision related to ethical reasoning requires emotional intelligence, which is gained from life experience and active learning. Individuals move through stages in their own lives as they mature that invariably moves them from a self-centred or fear-based reasoning to accordance with societal laws and rules and authority figures. At the highest stages of development, actions become more aligned with principled thought and individuals will consider universal justice and human rights in societal context. Fewer than 20 per cent of American adults reach the principled level where actions are consistent with moral thinking (Kohlberg, 1969).

Thus, if a manager's thinking about societal and environmental dilemmas is mostly a construct of external influences rather than personal conviction, then deciding what is right or wrong has more to do with reward systems, organizational leadership, work environment and peer group influence. This suggests that the organization has more effect on moral reasoning than does personal development.

Research has found that accounting practitioners have lower moral reasoning scores than counterparts in other professions, and that managers and partners in accounting firms have lower moral reasoning scores than those at lower organizational levels. Elm and Nichols (1993) found that older and tenured managers had lower scores than younger and less experienced employees. It may be that organizations an organizations work settings depress cognitive moral judgement processes. If this is the case, people with higher moral reasoning may be overlooked for leadership roles simply because they cannot ignore certain problems in their environment.

However, leaders with the right mix of business acumen and higher moral reasoning skills may be exactly what is needed for a productive cultural shift. Leaders who have the capacity for more complex systems thinking and moral reasoning can conceptualize problems in ways that go beyond self-interest and short-term gain. Leaders with lower levels of moral reasoning depress group performance and lower the group's average reasoning score (Trevino et al., 2006). Selecting an appropriate sponsor and manager for any program that requires cultural integration or social engagement should score relatively highly on a moral reasoning scale to obtain the necessary management dynamic.

But having a leader who can think in systems and reason complexity may not be enough. Organizations may have barriers in place related to playing a part in economic and social progress. Conduct in the workplace may be strictly regimented and self-regulating may lead to a moral disengagement. By morally disengaging, the individual is free to conduct activities that may conflict with one's personal ethical standards. This can happen in a few ways.

Individuals may justify their actions, blame other people or circumstances or distort the facts. In every case of moral disengagement is a relieving of personal responsibility. Workplaces that exhibit the characteristics of moral disengagement are more individualized, less cooperative, and corrupt. The biggest problem is that they may not see the problem. The cultural bias in place affects how information is processed and the resultant decision making. The organization could end up reducing 'risk or impact considerations' that would normally be part of a rational decision-making process thus increasing risk to itself. Utilizing stakeholders to help bring perspective and relieve the disengagement can help consciously expand the decision-making process to include potential consequences. Considering this, employing a CSR program could improve risk reduction strategy and re-engage the organization in an ethically progressive way.

There are many benefits to running an ethically inclined organization. We live better when we live a moral life. Integrating life decisions that align with one's moral beliefs have stronger commitment value and greater optimism. By subverting one's moral values, one, in effect, betrays oneself, and goals and dreams as well. Having models of ethical and fair behaviour in the workplace assist in developing character and attributes in co-workers to support social wellbeing and programs such as CSR. Although multiple social identities exist in the workplace, managers need to exhibit good character and model behaviour they wish to see to bring out the best in their workers and peers. Maintaining multiple social identities (spouse, worker, manager, friend) that do not align in values can create great stress in relationships and in working and home life. Want a happy workplace? Align your values and people towards a common goal.

The question of reward systems enters into how an organization can incent and align behaviour. Reward systems do not actually have an effect on ethical behaviour as they undermine the reasons for being ethical. People may also see unethical people being rewarded, which risks creating more of the same. Rewards systems need to be designed to be inclusive and peer-reviewed, must be well understood, and should look at the whole team for contribution. This way, an organization can marry the formal and informal cultures to align so ethical improvements are authentic.

Leadership for good and ethical business practice may not be solely placed on the executive. In fact, closer working relationships have more influence on peer behaviour, and role models can be found anywhere in the hierarchy. Finding champions for internal change that are involved with causes outside the workplace would assist in promoting your CSR, build public relations and involve your team in new beneficial ways of working. Social learning in the workplace needs to be an integral part of any organizational development plan. Language, modelling, and reciprocity are all part of the organizational culture and ethics within business needs to be part of an open exchange of ideas and communications. Authority figures need to take charge of the dialogue occurring in the organization, recognize the constraints and crack the quietness of sensitive topics or risk isolating individuals who feel topics are being ignored. One of the biggest mistakes a leader can make is to presume quietness means everything is all right.

By understanding that the integrity of the systems with which we operate in, directly impact the integrity of the organization, we start to dissolve the idea of separateness – that business exists in a vacuum apart from any outside influence. This division in the mind between business and nature is called externalization, and subverting our intrinsic values begins that alienation.

CSR can play a role in reintegrating values of community with those of business to the benefit of all. Togetherness or collaboration is nature's way of working it out. In nature, it perpetuates a symbiosis between life forms that works with the systems with which we integrate. One system helps, limits and maintains another within natural laws.

Because collaboration requires 'finding a way', 'making it work', 'not giving up' – people involved will be motivated to find the best way to move forward in all our common interests. The importance of

33

including stakeholders in collaborating yields a spectrum of expertise and opportunities to do better. In fact, it is natural to work in modes of collaboration and trust is the basis for such collaboration. The best partnerships are always the most collaborative and trustworthy. The best governments work with great people (and great people, hopefully, run for election). The best projects have the best working teams (and great teams come up with the best projects). We are always happiest when working in sync with each other rather than at odds with each other and there is a scientific basis to prove this. *If happiness is contagious than so are ethics.*

In an age when we need to collaborate to solve our global crisis, the touted market raison d'etre of rational self-interest sounds like an oxymoron. We need to raise business standards to meet our common expectations of the future.

The Psyche of Consumption

'If you chase two rabbits, you will lose them both' – Native American Saying

The above quotation highlights that a decision about our direction has to be made and acted upon. We looked at the ethical struggle that can occur within an organization. There is also a relationship between buyer and seller that can create ethical conflict as well. People, now labelled consumers, are driven by societal norms to behave in a repeated predicable pattern – receive stimulus from advert, get in car (or go online), exchange credit for debt, obtain product, go home, enjoy. Nowhere in the advert does it intimate that consideration for pollution or people's rights should guide your decision. This is understandable, we want things, we get them – just like children. The narcissism achieved from privatization privileges the 'me'. It is the modern *affluenza*. An understanding of why some consumers engage in unethical business may help us understand these relationships better and create a better CSR program to benefit both producer and consumer.

Consumer behaviour is engaged in acquisition, using and disposing of their purchases and as a sector, outdoes big business and government in damages to society and environment. Unethical consumer behaviour ranges from shoplifting to buying substances and products that are outlawed. It could also mean pirating software, purchasing counterfeits, or creating a monopoly. This may be because of consumer awareness or lack thereof; there are no perceivable alternatives or artefacts in their belief system that foresees consequences in their actions. Such belief systems are also associated with self-destructive behaviour.

There is a lack of an evaluative structure in consumer thinking, creating a more reactive behaviour rather than a thoughtful process. In this type of acquisition, an individual may be seeking to raise their status or illegitimately gain resources to increase their satisfaction levels appealing to a low level of consciousness. In other cases, it is about presumed responsibility.

An unethical action may be taken because it is assumed that another person should have caught or fixed a flawed process. However, it turns out people perceive the impacts of their actions more often when they are associated with positive consequences (Vitell et al, 2001). To be fair, this is not every consumer, it is a set of people who act solely in their own self-interest with no regard for others. Policing this type of behaviour is not possible, it will be societal and cultural norms that will influence and dictate penalties associated with unethical behaviour. Reward systems should recognize decent, honest customers who contribute to the betterment of business and community relationships, another area that an organized CSR program can be of great benefit.

Because the consumer sector is so damaging to the environment, individuals and consumers must change or have change impressed upon them as we approach ecological limits. The consumer economy is in a state of transition from which it cannot return, and the death of the industrial age is coming simply because continuance with the current waste and by-product issues are not an option. At our current rate of using one and a half earth's worth of bioproductivity, our footprint is outgrowing the earth's recuperative abilities. Just looking at the state of the oil-based economy demands a total shift in the way we consume and thus produce. We have actually been transitioning to a new age for some time: the Information Economy.

The changes to business and society have been monumental, yet has managed to escape what the majority of people view as a new paradigm. It has changed the way we do business, organize ourselves in most of our daily routines, connect with our communities and even changed the face of politics. The internet networking model is now a standard form of human organization and has been birthed in symbols and language such as social media, social marketing, tweeting, etc. We have adopted the information age with open arms, and have yet to embrace it to tackle the biggest problems in society today. Social innovators are the first among a breed of do-gooders leveraging technology and partnerships to solve societal problems.

There are signs that consumer consciousness around environmental impacts of purchasing and consumption are growing. Consumers are working with businesses and government to recycle and reuse packaging and secure damaging elements form electronics from leaking into the environment. Since 2006, producers are required to register before putting electronic products on the German market. When registering for household electronics, they are required to provide a guarantee to ensure the financing of the proper disposal of electrical and electronic equipment placed on the market. At the same time, a coordinated and comprehensive household waste separation program involves industry with the recollection of materials they use. This has the effect of forcing industry to think in design terms about their own production and waste cycles, creating greater efficiency and much less waste.

But are we ready for post-industrialization? Are we ready for a drastic reduction in consumption and a greater involvement in communication? The coming revolution will not be lead by leaders of companies but by communities and networks of people that include those leaders; a true collaboration.

Unless we are organized and have planned for the change, no amount of desire will allow it to happen smoothly and successfully. It takes a bottom-up approach to create this kind of change. When was the last time a monarchy led a revolution? People can be defined as either being an activist or inactivist, and it is the only the former that creates change. Moving forward we will shed the skin of the industrial age and move to a more conscious healthy lifestyle that will uphold our responsibilities to our peers, families and communities. This will change the face of consumerism for society and business in ways we are already seeing.

The transition may be psychologically painful for those reliant on materialism as a lifestyle. Any change in habits has associated withdrawal symptoms. Anyone attached emotionally to the individual consumption and disposal patterns constructed by the dig, consume and burn psychology of the industrial age will have a difficult time adjusting in times of resource scarcity or cooperative sharing. But the resulting clean-tech age or resource awareness age, will be a step that humanity will be taking for a more positive and healthy future and business has a role. Business can be other than that which circles the drain and spirals downward into tragedy. It can be a catalyst for new relationships, for developing a new consumer and as a source of inspiration and education while creating commerce for improving living everywhere.

We are moving from a false belief of limitless resources and endless push for human labour productivity as a civilizational meme to an understanding of natural systems, limitations and resource productivity, to a much more responsible mode of being. The world is not limited provided we work within the principles of life and the physics of regenerative life giving properties. The earth provides everything we need, materials, nutrients and riches for our quality of living for as long as we respect and care for our surroundings. There are endless things to discover about our home before we trash it. But not trashing it is going to take a big leap in faith and changing the way we relate to each other. Just as personal changes will happen, relationships between groups, countries and business will all have to adjust.

But just knowing where we need to go is not enough. There needs to be a plan and action with leadership and management of cultural

37

significance. Influencers, motivators and executors all need to champion a CSR program and drive it home in the hearts and minds of the organization. The culture shift is necessary because large groups may stultify progress falling back on out-dated habits and social norms that are counter-productive.

Business will resist change because their thinking does not allow them to see the dynamics of new enterprise that includes society and environment. Consumers may even manipulate or seek to take advantage of a business treading a new path. In consumer psychology, they may justify trying to 'rip off the system' when they see large gross profits in an age of austerity or when executives are rewarded with huge sums of money and workers are barely keeping up with raises in inflation. Greed surely works both ways. Remember, businesses are composed of a labour force of consumers. But how do businesses justify manipulating consumers?

Understanding What Influences People

Any attempt to alter a culture of an organization or to have influence over or with other groups must include a discussion and analysis of the social structures and psyche of the individuals making up that group. Group influence and communications have conscious and unconscious behavioural altering effects that must be understood in context of making improvements that benefit both business and society. To truly develop an encompassing organizational change program using CSR it must require commitment and understanding.

Businesses and media have a large influence on social norms. Corporate advertising is specifically aimed at triggering responses in an individual by appealing to subconscious mechanisms. Our consumer society depends on these reactions and desires. The promotion of a consumptive behaviour does not stop at the checkout but continues into the lifestyle. Certainly, media suggests consuming our way to success will make us happy but research suggests a different picture.

One in five Americans experiences mental illness every year. These statistics are rising while budgets for treating such disorders are being slashed. Homeless people have substantially higher rates of mental illness. In 2008, the Conference of Mayors reported a substantial increase in homelessness numbering at least 1.5 million over two years. This includes one out of every 50 children. This is related to lack of affordable housing, poverty and unemployment and can include issues such as drug abuse and mental illness. Veterans are also a large portion of homelessness, as many suffer from experiencing the atrocities of violence and war.

All of this exists as we continue to chase a spiral staircase of consumerism. Apparently, buying our way to happiness, even in the richest country in the world, does not work. But there is evidence to suggest that just having enough is the key to living a good life.

Nobel Laureate Daniel Kahneman has produced a large amount of amazing research on subjective well being examining quality of life factors. This includes individual and socially contextual feelings and perceptions. Comparisons were done between appraisals in one's life about the utility of materials items against other factors such as relationships. What becomes apparent is that there is an illusion that more income would make us happier. People tend to overestimate or overstate the value that more income would bring to their lives. "The belief that high income is associated with good mood is widespread but mostly illusory," the researchers wrote (Science magazine 2006). "People with above-average income are relatively satisfied with their lives but are barely happier than others in moment-to-moment experience, tend to be more tense, and do not spend more time in particularly enjoyable activities."

Researchers examined data from a nationwide Bureau of Labor Statistics to show that people with higher incomes devote relatively more of their time to work, shopping, childcare and other 'obligatory' activities. Women surveyed by the researchers in Ohio associated those activities with "higher tension and stress." People with higher incomes spend less time on "passive leisure" activities such as socializing or watching television, which the respondents viewed as more enjoyable. For example, to earn more money someone may accept a long commute, which is among the top worst moments of the day for people. The moods and attitudes associated with a less than happy life permeate into the business culture. Although people do not speak or illicit these feelings at work, they are there and have a profound effect on everything from decision making to group meetings.

The study of hedonics is literally the study of happiness. What makes one happy or content is a subjective experience but there are common elements we all have that bring us mental and physical wellbeing. This has implications for organizations in terms of reward systems or recognition for good work done. For reward systems to be most effective, they should appeal not just to a desire for material accumulation but to core values, where the heart of positive motivation lies. Those who are responsible for managing reward systems may want to consider the value of time over money when delivering incentives. It turns out that those who have more time and spend it on rewarding activities are happier than those who have money.

Corporate social responsibility can easily expand to become corporate psychological responsibility when considering the power of influence a CSR program could have if designed with culture in mind. Group influence within organizations manifests itself in the informal culture – that side of the organization that contains all the gossip, values, dreams that people would like to express formally but cannot or is deemed improper in the formal culture. The implications for a positive psychology approach using CSR are increases in productivity, loyalty, and improved relationships.

Consenting To Dissent

Many traditions in organizations continue without a cultural examination to the detriment of the organization. One such tradition is the business meeting. One way which meetings and group assembly influences people towards the lowest common denominator is a process called 'groupthink'. Groupthink results in making poor decisions and commitment to a losing course of action. Essentially, small groups revert to a sluggish blob where critical thinking is lost and individual differences are subverted. Basically, the group goes brain dead because the culture does not allow for dissent or free expression. This mindlessness is wholly inadequate for dealing with emerging issues. There are many social and psychological reasons for this. Some of these include: maintaining a positive image of the group; lack of desire to participate; lack of good leadership emergence process; false sense of safety; fear of anxiety or being outcast; masking of powerlessness and confusion.

Getting though a business meeting does not require courage and initiative. Introverts may also not be able to express in meetings due to the 'loud mouth' or attention seekers. Examining and understanding the way people group and communicate within the organization will allow for cultural assessment and change management initiatives to target for improvements. Openness and encouragement of expression can combat the narrowness or rigidity of the organizational framework – it must be safe to express all of one's thoughts. Open up to vulnerability and allow for the power of criticism and questioning to be part of the process. Indeed, there is a role for the dissenter to improve conditions and open minds to innovation. This type of dissention or disruption can be a powerful creative force and productive generator of ideas leading to new ways of doing things. But this requires a manager who understands how to work and facilitate these types of sessions.

To delve a little deeper, groups of people behave quite differently than individuals. It is human organization that manages to be less than the sum of its parts by castrating the creative process. When people engage in meetings, their priority is to manage anxiety by deploying social defences that distort the ability to think and act creatively (Elmes, 1990). This illusion that things are under control masks true thoughts and feelings. In times of contradictory feeling or conflict, the more energy goes into the defence mechanisms. This can be physically and emotionally draining. Thus, what is unreal takes precedence over that which is real. The group will also create the myth of a 'great leader', relying on management or leadership to solve issues using the creativity and expression that they themselves want. Unless there is an intervention, members will continue to distort reality to calm their fears and falsely believe in a leader.

41

The leader-member relationship can take on a child like dependence as critical thinking is renounced for false security. Again, we see an infantilization process, not based on consumption desires, but to assuage fear and insecurity. They leave the critical thinking, the exploratory process, the inquiry and vision to the leader of the group, reducing any potential and purpose for the group to gather at all. By investing so much in the leader, a group can be dismembered when the leader fails and the illusion comes crashing. Dissent never becomes an option even when processes, plans or the environment comes crashing down around them.

Dissent can be a fearful exercise in itself. To express feelings and thoughts that create doubt in a group can be uncomfortable and stir thoughts that question the leader and organization itself. But dissenters are the ones who have the ability to modify a group's frame of reference and introduce new methods of problem-solving. Dissenters simply want to introduce intellectual or emotional differences so that what may be thought and not expressed, is expressed.

Social networks combined with information technology can create adhocracies – groups of people with common values and interests that form a communications network to potentially organize an information campaign. Information campaigns, if done properly, can lead to a change in attitude and behaviour. Mass media does this all the time, engineering consent. Now social media is surpassing broadcasting as we Tweet, use Facebook, and blog our values-based campaigns around the world. Businesses have realized the huge potential to tap into these networks to influence consumer behaviour through adverts and selective marketing, creating web sites worth billions. But they are only measuring the monetary worth. The social worth is much more valuable, especially in terms of creating a transition to collaborative networks. Many companies have now taken to allowing employees full access to online social networking sites.

Delving Deeper

Corporate organizations are no exception. There is no wealth without health and so the structure of the organization must be re-engineered for economic, social and environmental performance rather than a profit centre alone. Without a greater purpose, the organization exists only as a compliance mechanism to shareholders, treating workers like children and automatons instead of intelligent self-thinking adults whose combined potential could change the world.

Further examining the psychology of an organization operating on obligation from employees alone, we can trace the roots of the mediocrity. Alan Durning cites economist Victor Lebow who summed up the ethics of the consumer nation in the post-war era quite nicely in the 1950s:

> Our enormously productive economy ... demands that we make consumption our way of life, that we convert the buying and the selling of goods into rituals, that we seek our spiritual satisfaction, our ego satisfaction in commodities...We need things consumed, burned up, worn out, replaced, and discarded at an ever-increasing rate (Durning, 1992, p. 21).

From that quote, the line differentiating consumer and citizen has been blurred. Lebow is suggesting that our physical and psychic energies be devoted to using up produced goods as quickly as possible, clearly with no remorse for social or environmental consequences. Where 'citizen' means being a responsible community member and contributor to good order and evolution of society, 'consumer' replaces the ethic with a material production model that is more individualistic and negates responsibility. The primary drivers of behaviour and good living look more like commercials than the need for innovation, social progress and strong community.

So how do we grow up and assume our responsibilities as organizations for betterment of society? Upon examination of the consumer ethic, we can see why the rise of private goals over public good has become engrained in the our culture – individualism over community and thus personal desires over society and environment, the consequences of which are compounding interest daily. This is the basis of all modern economic theory, that individual self-interest and utilitarian philosophy drive consumption to produce trade. We must be capable of producing trade in a much more responsible fashion: after all we have split the atom and visited the moon.

Convenience and freedom of choice have become priorities in our lives at home and creep into work. We cannot be bothered to separate waste or make an extra trip or bring our own mug to the local coffee shop. The same applies to a workplace because you cannot separate the ethic. People at work will use more supplies, take more unnecessary trips, and leave equipment switched overnight, wasting energy. You can bet these habits do not change at home.

The constant bombardment of advertising teaches us it is socially advantageous to own an expensive car and house, to self-express through what you own rather than what you are inside, constructing our identities as we buy. With our 'dowry', we then can attract the supermodels of our dreams, fulfilling all our desires. This is really an emotional plea to the ego and self-image rather than a solution to life's challenges. The constant bombardment of the top one per cent flaunting their lifestyles at us through television and media, can create the illusion that we may all obtain the same lifestyle, which is simply untrue and would be unsustainable. This flaunting is nothing more than an attempt to manufacture material desire and requires our emotional buy-in. The truth is, people taking more than they need are no happier than you or I, and there is substantial research to support this.

So how does this relate to creating a socially responsible organization? Our emotions get involved in making everyday decisions. Social and psychological triggers are consistently used to get us to 'buy-in' to a product or pitch. You can understand the rise in ethical purchasing like fair trade and organics as we become aware of our connections. These same triggers are at work in working life, in the clubs you go to, in the social venues. What can create a difference is the communication or expression of social values in our every day lives. Issues regarding health and safety, or community involvement must be allowed to be expressed or suffer the mediocrity of group think.

Because we tend to focus on a narrow perspective of progress, we are now embedded deeper into continuing poor courses of action and reinforcing patterns of behaviour that we know are resulting in poor performance. Fear of change maintains status quo behaviour, even when faced with a dilemma, humans will repeat patterns based on 'group think'. Group think is characterized by the loss of creativity and independent thinking as the group struggles to obtain cohesiveness, thereby losing the motivation to appraise alternative courses of action - what Vandana Shiva refers to as a 'monoculture of the mind'.

In psychology, the material consumption patterns can be contrasted to the Maslow's hierarchy of needs. Such behavioural specialists as Clayton Alderfer, and David McClelland, whose theories have shaped human resource and diversity management, have formed the basis for organizational development and human resource functions throughout the world.

To simplify, the hierarchy of needs are arranged from lowest to highest, the lowest being physiological needs such as food, water, shelter. As these needs are met, a psychological evolution occurs and one can now pursue the meeting of the next order, which is safety and security. The highest order need to be met is called 'self-actualization' and is characterized by personal growth and achievement and generally by taking the form of teacher or model for others. This makes sense when we look at the way many cultures have evolved to keep elders as their teachers and council, transferring knowledge to those younger in the community, influencing norms of behaviour that reinforce progress and transgressing rites of passage.

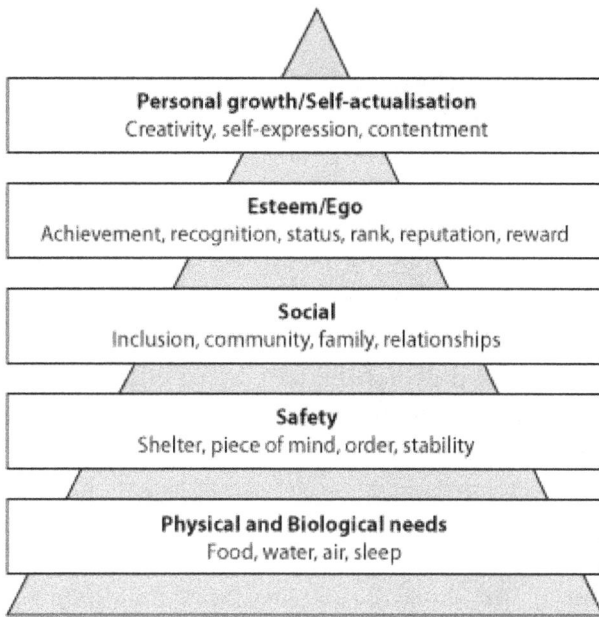

Personal growth/Self-actualisation	Creativity, self-expression, contentment
Esteem/Ego	Achievement, recognition, status, rank, reputation, reward
Social	Inclusion, community, family, relationships
Safety	Shelter, piece of mind, order, stability
Physical and Biological needs	Food, water, air, sleep

In western society purporting a productivity ethic, we hide the old and infirm away because they are no longer productive units of the economy and our youth are now growing more lost, with few rites of passage and little direction to bring them to maturity. In this way, the economy is an oppressive function of society. Certainly, the economy has reduced our personal interaction with nature. Designing urban centres for commerce rather than ecosystem interaction has results in a number of diseases, pollution issues, habitat destruction and even mental illness. In what Richard Louv shows in *Last Child in the Woods* as **nature deficit disorder**, children who have reduced exposure to nature have higher incidence of Attention Deficit Disorder. The problem is so great that government and educational policy is now being made to ensure children interact with nature.

In March 2007, the New Mexico State Legislature approved the Outdoor Classrooms Initiative, an effort to increase outdoor education in the state. Later, Washington governor Christine Gregoire signed into law the *Leave No Child Inside* initiative, legislation that allocates $1.5 million a year to outdoor programs working with underserved children. In California, similar legislation has been introduced to fund long-term outdoor education and recreation programs serving at-risk youth. All of this is recognition of our deeper connection to nature and a realization that nature must be included in all our decision making. But we don't actually have a youth problem, we have an adult problem.

Economy is only a system of human behaviour, it does not exist otherwise. Therefore should we not ensure that our behaviour is responsible and for mutual benefit? The lack of attention to personal development from youth through working years has left us with a large population of non-actualized people, resulting in immature managers and management practices with no idea of thinking in complex and deep issues related to societal progress or in empathizing with team members who struggle with personal conflicts.

Understanding motivational factors should be common science for managers. There are four levels of analysis from which motivation have been examined: (a) physiological, which is concerned with the brain's control of motivated states; (b) individual, targeting motivational changes that occur as a result of internal or external conditions; (c) social, which is based on the premise that a person's behaviour tends to change when he or she is in the company of others; and (d) philosophical, which results when the analysis is based upon the theorists' philosophies rather than empirical data (Petri, 1986).

We may approach people more deeply to understand the desires and motivations that are less selfish and more altruistic. This is where we find the most motivating, creative and passionate part of ourselves. Leaders can learn how to tap into this almost limitless resource within their own organization.

Unconscious Consumerism

Individuals are entrenched with a consumer ethic in that it keeps an individual cycling in the meeting of the lower order of needs – 'I want'. Consumers need no longer grow up and develop their intellectual and spiritual potential when they identify with a material item that can quickly be discarded and done over again. This short-term thinking has infantilized adult society.

Thinking in money and materialism promotes different behaviour than when an individual is conscious about time and relationships. In a time-conscious individual, one is more apt to spend time socializing with loved ones and acquiring experiences, and is healthier for it. All of this highlights the need for maturity and emotional intelligence when approaching the problems of business and the environment. Psychology and our mental wellbeing is integral to success, a portion of our existence that has fallen out of priority to accumulation. Hopefully we can raise the next generation to think differently, but that will necessitate a proactive approach.

The desire for monetary gain knows no limits and requires no morals, creating an extremely predatory activity. Children are often the targets of consumer campaigns. Their tastes and opinions drive market trends. Traditional teaching methods cannot compete with the appeal of a commercial world of games that make heroes out of children or puts the fate of Harry Potter at their hands (Barber, 2007).

Driving desire in children means appealing to their egos. It is a universal marketing strategy with all children everywhere, regardless of culture, that they can relate to the same basic needs, whereas adults are much more pluralistic. As Dr. David Jones and Doris Klein wrote over 35 years ago, "the child wants what it wants when it wants it, without consideration of the needs of others, and man-child does not outgrow this pattern." (2007, p. 18). These children grow up to perhaps manage people some day. Now imagine how a team of people feel when this condition is recognized in an adult, a manager, that has control over the quality of their working lives.

Thus, consumer behaviour patterns require infantilization to maintain the state of desiring things, to supersede adult concerns or dilemmas such as environment or community, by satisfying immediate desires, and as a result, must be suppressed from reaching higher order intellectualism. Now we can understand why egos are self-interested and fail to become guides and problem solvers for the communities in which they belong, they simply cannot see the systems of which they are a part. They are infantilized by their own personal desires, caught up in immaturity on the inside, while showing poise on the outside. In the most superficial manner, the outside persona is kept to fulfil the inside ego. In psychology, this is narcissism and is a prominent attribute in material societies.

We see the influence of immaturity in our media. Commercials are great at depicting adults looking like children with their new products in hand, some even dancing with cartoon characters. Without delving too deeply into the psychology of consumer behaviour, a conclusion can be reached that being locked in these patterns keeps individuals from moving to higher order states of being and thus higher order contentment.

The ability to reflect deeply and think critically is out of reach for the material addict who is the prime target for the psychology of persuasion. While some seek empowerment from the shopping mall, others acquire feelings of self-efficacy through changing the world for the better. This simplistic view is admittedly polarized, not everyone who goes to the mall is brain dead, but the point must be made about what roles we aspire to be playing as we development in the workplace and in our communities. In a sweeping change, people are re-determining what factors are important in life satisfaction.

Dr. Robert Cialdini, a social psychologist, has written the successful book, *Influence: The Psychology of Persuasion*. He highlights six powerful 'weapons of persuasion' that he insists are powerful because of the discombobulating of our lives. We are more likely to use less information for making decisions due to increased stress, fatigue and limits to cognitive resources. By relying on quick cues or singular pieces of information that generally guide us in our daily living we can cope with the bombardment of stimulus. However, if those cues are manipulated or ill timed, we can make stupid mistakes that can be exploited by others.

I will summarize Cialdini's six methods of persuasion and you may begin to see why as individuals and organizations, we are failing to be more effective at making progress. The six methods are:

Reciprocation – the feeling of indebtedness that is used to create a giving back behaviour. We often become obliged to others by receiving something for nothing.

Commitment and Consistency – a person whose expressed values and actions don't match is deemed indecisive or two-faced. Good personal consistency is valued in a culture and we automatically fall into behaviours that keep us in accord. Being consistent is good for avoiding change. Making a commitment in public or in writing carries more weight and personal obligation because of social consequences.

Social Proof – the behaviour of a group of which we are a part, alters our own norms of behaviour. This can lead to synchronous action or inaction as is the case with bystanders at an accident. Everyone is looking to everyone else for social cues on how to behave in a situation until one breaks the line.

Liking – we respond with greater compliance when it is from someone we know and like. This also works if requests are made from someone physically attractive or someone who is like ourselves in looks and demeanour. Attractive models are often used to sell products.

Authority – we are taught from a young age to follow order and rule. Order brings great advantages to a society for such things as development and growth, but if authority is misused, it can be oppressive.

Scarcity – we will comply in a situation where an opportunity appears to have limited availability or if it seems socially desirable. We rush to get a piece of the action before it is gone.

All of these points are used by advertising in department stores, newsprint and television to great effect but less so in the social progress arena. Consider a commercial, the characters in it, what the messages are and compare to the above points. You are being asked to comply but on levels that we are not usually cognitively aware of –

essentially being manipulated. So if we are too busy to think about what direction we are heading as an organization or society, we are probably susceptible to the short-term, reactive type of thinking that plagues our communities and current planning practices.

Organizations may not even realize how divided they are internally as the division mindset may be so entrenched. The informal organization exists apart from the bureaucracy and has a culture all of its own. The competitiveness that is supposed to be the philosophy behind successful free market distribution is less effective than a collaborative economy and a basic psychological experiment – boys at a summer camp - shows us why.

Looking at divisive social attitudes, such as racism, gender bias or any other type of differentiator, we see a problem with integration. There is an assumption that greater exposure to another group will create tolerance, but this isn't the case. The conditions under which groups are exposed to each other determines the relationship.

Social scientist Muzafer Sherif performed an experiment with a boys' summer camp. Unbeknownst to them, the boys were being observed under conditions that would induce rival behaviour. From the start, the boys were divided into two camps or teams and asked to define themselves as such with a name and logo. It was found that to start disharmony and create rivalry. All you had to do was separate the participants into two groups and leave them be. The real premise to the experiment was how to unify them once the hostility was embedded within.

The experiments were constructed in such a way as to create self-interest, thereby creating a competitive attitude and behaviour. The exercises would only benefit everyone if they found a way to work together. After a series of slurs, insults and even scuffles, the groups were then posed with challenges that required a joint effort. The boys found that by working together they were able to get a bus unstuck from the mud, pool their money to rent movies for movie night and help distribute water when the generator was down. Once a cooperative relationship was established the boys took an affinity to one another and began to share their own resources with the others,

51

taking no more than they needed. Self-interest was dissolved and a well-formed community was happier and more productive for it.

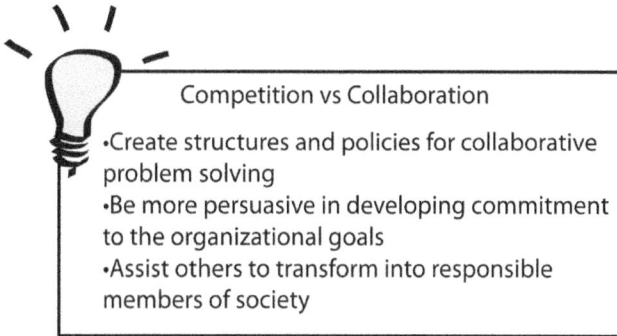

Competition vs Collaboration

•Create structures and policies for collaborative problem solving
•Be more persuasive in developing commitment to the organizational goals
•Assist others to transform into responsible members of society

So what is all the divisiveness and competition in the world doing to us as a community? We end up wasting natural and intellectual resources, start bitter rivalries and lose social capital. Any resemblance of this experiment to partisan politics and corporate competitive behaviour is not strictly coincidental.

Perhaps the corporation, as an organization, should have a strategy for collaboration and social capital building as their *Intention Statement.* Corporate responsibilities are not in proportion with the overall social power that it exerts. Organizations would do well to empower their employees into learning modes that bring out their full talent and potential, allowing them to realize who they are as mature and compassionate adults and create contributing workers towards organizational and societal goals.

CSR can play a role in facilitating the attainment of higher order needs within the organization and assist in the consciousness raising. As a consultant or coach, a good way to approach CSR and new thinking is to develop engaging modules and exercises for employees or even to do personal awareness and leadership sessions. Posing corporate problems in such a way as to be a collaborative and group effort will yield economic and social benefits.

Given the nature of an amoral market, we surely will never rid ourselves completely of corporate manipulation or consumers trying to rip people off. Rather, it will be up to us to adopt new lifestyles and modes of organization to meet our future needs of health and redefining prosperity.

Measuring New Behaviour

"Too much and too long, we seem to have surrendered community excellence and community values in the mere accumulation of material things. Our gross national product ... if we should judge America by that - counts air pollution and cigarette advertising, and ambulances to clear our highways of carnage. It counts special locks for our doors and the jails for those who break them. It counts the destruction of our redwoods and the loss of our natural wonder in chaotic sprawl. It counts napalm and the cost of a nuclear warhead, and armored cars for police who fight riots in our streets. It counts Whitman's rifle and Speck's knife, and the television programs which glorify violence in order to sell toys to our children…

Yet the gross national product does not allow for the health of our children, the quality of their education, or the joy of their play. It does not include the beauty of our poetry or the strength of our marriages; the intelligence of our public debate or the integrity of our public officials. It measures neither our wit nor our courage; neither our wisdom nor our learning; neither our compassion nor our devotion to our country; it measures everything, in short, except that which makes life worthwhile. And it tells us everything about America except why we are proud that we are Americans." - Robert F. Kennedy Address, University of Kansas, Lawrence, Kansas, March 18, 1968

Much of our daily lives and decisions we make are based on our psychological wellbeing, our world views, much of it influenced through constricted media channels. Without the right attitudes and

53

information, decisions in organizations can be poorly made or influenced by seemingly innocuous intentions. Reliance on such information channels can be dangerous when the need to address real world issues must be made. With even a basic understanding of priorities, we can take alternate perspectives and begin to set new goals, measuring performance in new and beneficial ways and taking responsibility for our roles to see progress.

We naturally take note of how things are progressing in our daily lives all the time. Rather than comparing ourselves to others, we will measure our own well being and purpose as an organization and then share in the discovery and best practices. We do this appraisal process constantly to check ourselves, where we are at to where we want to and should be. We do this to see how we are doing towards a collaborative vision of a better world. The same appraisal needs to happen in balance with organizations, business, and communities. A new approach based on contemplation, strategy and surgical execution will replace reaction, doubt, and repetition.

Business transactions take place in the social sphere of trade, exchanging goods and services, using the tools of currency to mark the amounts and balances. All of this is done under the guise that trading is meant to improve quality of life, if it does not or does so for the few at the expense of the many, then we need to ask why are we doing it? The economy does not look at the costs of production and related social impacts, or the deforestation associated with a product, or the pollution downstream created in the process of the manufacturing. These costs are deferred or passed on, immediately to someone or something else, typically the health care system or the ecosystem, eventually returned as lower environmental air or water quality and reduction in ability to support biodiversity and life itself.

CSR and the connections for financial performance need to be measured and understood by management. There are typical justifications for a business case in support of developing a CSR:

- Value of a good reputation and stakeholder perception
- Cost reductions and operating efficiencies
- Better risk management

- Competitive advantage through product differentiating and/or premium pricing ability
- Reducing the threat of burdensome regulation
- Opening new markets
- Improving employee motivation
- Reducing anti-business campaigns
- Introducing new technologies
- Enhancing local quality of life for employee retention (Donna J. Wood, 2010)

These are just some of the internal benefits, but as we have already touched on, the external benefits are available as well.

The above points are proactive and require adaptation with respect to management behaviour in creating CSR. If left too late, regulation may force business to internalize social and environmental costs, costing more to upgrade and develop a knowledge base in the long-term making the business less competitive. For example, carbon management is increasingly becoming a monitored and regulated substance due to its impacts and potential for global warming. If we wait for regulation we have missed the point. The risk here is that we enter an enforcement era, where saving the environment becomes and eco-fascism of sorts and business begins to run out of choices as do consumers and clients. When everything becomes regulated we lose freedom in choice and direction of resource use, thus we must be proactive in saving plenty of resources for our future. Business in a twist, can become a proponent of democracy by properly managing its operations so that more choices become available in the future.

Evaluating Progress

What gets measured gets managed - sometimes. This is true provided the observations are relevant and valid to the goals of the organization and its stakeholders and that there is a competent management structure to follow through on policy related to the feedback. The selection of indicators reflects the broad and specific business objectives and informs as to the progress and direction of efforts. However, there must be allowance for the unknown or unpredictable and for ignorance in human decision making. This is called the Precautionary Principal and although not mandatory, is a philosophy that will bring us back from the brink of ecosystem failure. Using this approach, we could eliminate harmful impacts before we begin production but again, we need to be educated and informed.

The quality of information to assist in making decisions is crucial and is grossly underestimated in many organizations. Some indicators are widely used yet do not accurately reflect the state of affairs. For example, the GDP or Gross Domestic Product, measures the economic productivity of a nation but cannot tell us about the health of its citizens or the quality of its rivers. The GDP for the United States actually rose to reflect the damage and work done on cleanup from the Exxon oil spill on the Alaskan coastline, indicating economic improvement because of the work generated, but all the real costs will be borne by the region for many years to come.

Although some may be critical of CSR benefits, the link to financial and market performance is obvious when a firm's negative impacts are known. A business is noticed when it harms the natural environment, harms other local business, has poor labour practices or working conditions, is dishonest, offensive or unfair. These types of business activities have a direct negative impact on stock value, consumer confidence and willingness to buy again. Measuring progress also includes measuring reputation and ethical practices.

Can a working organization be a place of productivity, happiness, and of doing good? Should it not be then that the workplace environment naturally becomes the most talented, motivational, inspirational and productive place to be in one's life? Yet for many it is a place of mediocrity, valueless, and built on obligatory status. Human values are becoming more esoteric as people question if they are fulfilling their life's purpose. People measure themselves in much different ways than a business would. Examining and aligning values of success and discovering the opportunities for doing so is a win-win outcome. Developing new knowledge changes our focus and work efforts – we move towards what we study. Thus adopting new indicators, should in theory (and provided management is serious about progress), create new knowledge, workflows and refocus efforts into the much needed territory of sustainability. The learning begins when we open our eyes and minds to new possibilities and find our true purpose and there is no reason that the working organization should not be a facilitator of human progress.

In an effort to re-evaluate progress, many new indices have been developed and reporting agencies have adopted 'wellbeing' indicators. It is noteworthy to know that Bhutan has measured their nation with the Gross National Happiness indicator for years. The Prime Ministers job is to keep everyone reasonably happy, if he or she succeeds then they keep their job, if not, they are ousted. Makes sense.

North America has been experiencing a growth spurt in responsible reporting requirements for sustainable development, but mostly voluntarily with little standards in organizational adoption or reporting. In contrast to the conventional narrow focus on economic indicators, wellbeing reports require governments to directly and regularly measure people's subjective wellbeing: their experiences, feelings and perceptions of how their lives are going, as a new way of assessing societal progress. This is a learning process as the society is moving from the 'GDP means good' for everyone, to understanding that quality of life is not the same for everyone and wellness is a proactive endeavour. Here are a few:

- The Australian Unity Wellbeing Index
- New Zealand Family Wellbeing Indicators Report - http://www.stats.govt.nz/publications/standardofliving/family-wellbeing-indicators-report.aspx
- National Accounts of Wellbeing - http://www.nationalaccountsofwellbeing.org/
- Quality of life in a Changing Europe - http://projectquality.org/

These indicators and related studies include assessments of education, health and community, much the same type of information that is important to employers, but throughout it all is the theme of creating new knowledge and making relationships between previously disparate data sources for better decision-making.

57

The Rosetan Lifestyle

I wanted to bring to light that communities, which are a form of organization, can adopt functionality and customs for a healthier lifestyle. Evidence is surfacing daily that quality of life is more related to social factors than anything else. The United States is the wealthiest country in the world but has the highest depression rate. It also has the highest incarceration rate. Not the types of indicators we expect for a successful organization. But communities can show us how we can operate differently for the success of all.

To highlight the connection between wellbeing and social connections, Malcolm Gladwell points out a specific community with an interesting history in his book *Outliers*. I recap the story here, but recommend you indulge in reading the whole passage. The book opens with a description of the old town of Roseto Valfortore, southeast of Rome. This was a working town, close knit with a sense of community. Some townsfolk left to immigrate to America in the winter of 1882, hearing of the great opportunities. Word spread quickly and soon there were 1200 applicants for American passports. Eventually, the old town was virtually abandoned.

The Rosetans settled near a town called Bangor in Pennsylvania, buying up land and building their community on the rocky foothills. They built in the old traditions and maintained their culture to the point that their new town, now called Roseto, was all Italian speaking. Something was different about this town and for much different circumstances than one would suspect.

It was now the 1950s and Stewart Wolf, a physician and researcher in the study of heart disease, had heard from his fellows that this town, amidst an American heart-disease epidemic, was flourishing. He decided to setup a clinic and do research, testing the Rosetans for their blood chemistry and heart health. The results were astounding. Virtually no one under the age of fifty-five had died of a heart attack and for men over sixty-five it was half that of the whole of the United States. Aside from good health, they had no suicide, no alcoholism, no drug addiction, and little crime. They were dying of old age and that was all.

The town of Roseto is an outlier, according to Malcom Gladwell. They cooked with lard, ate fat, didn't exercise more than normal. Having eliminated diet, exercise and genes, Stewart Wolf had nowhere else to look for the reason for their long healthy lives, until it dawned on him. He examined their social practices. It seemed that when the Rosetans transplanted themselves from Italy they brought their social norms with them. These norms included frequent visitations, stopping in the street to chat with community members, cooking for one another and inviting people over for meals. The social interaction and camaraderie of community had extended into their lives. Many of the homes had extended families and gathered regularly at community events and at Sunday Mass. They discouraged the flaunting of capital and helped the unsuccessful obscure their failures. This was a social community.

It seemed that the culture of the Rosetan's had insulated themselves from the pressures of the modern world, creating a protective nurturing environment for their members. This kept them happy and healthy. Needless to say the medical establishment at the time rejected social factors in longevity, because no one was used to thinking about health in terms of community. Modern living has us believe that generating more wealth will keep us healthy. The values we hold have a profound effect on us and the people we surround ourselves with.

Now, there is overwhelming evidence to show that culture, or the elements of a culture can make or break an organization or community. Just as Stewart Wolf needed to change the minds of the medical community and show them they needed to change the way they approached health, we need to address our own institutions and change the way we think about life and community. We can gauge ourselves by the progress of the communities and organizations development, not just how much we consume. If social change is shown to be as beneficial to health and productivity as is shown, then the economic benefits are already there.

Measuring social performance can help top managers, board directors and other stakeholders understand if management is building valuable

59

long-term relationships and assets (Chatterji & Levine, 2006). Using short-term measurements can devalue hard-to-measure assets like relationships, employee skills and customer loyalty. "The goal of non-financial performance measurement is to align managerial incentives with long-term shareholder value and to better align shareholder value creation with social value creation." (ibid, 31). Also, the impact of high performance work practices (HPWP) on organizational performance has been given greater study in recent years and reveals that HPWP can be influential because they increase the knowledge skills and abilities of employees, are motivational, and empowering (Sniderman & Nelson, 2007).

With CSR an organization can be inclusive of a new set of indicators that have greater meaning, right down to the sociability. Return on investment takes on a longer term and more comprehensive perspective as we consider the health of our communities and the interests of the families of the members of our organizations. Wellbeing is the ultimate goal and the reason we work in the first place. How many of us would work a job we don't like if it did not pay for us to provide a life of security, leisure and experiences? And how many of us would work extra hard for an organization that looked after the needs of our families and recognized health and wellbeing in our lives – striking the work-life balance in a harmonious and mutually beneficial way? We can create a much different scenario than the prospects we are facing should we proceed on our current path.

Leading The Change

Employing robust CSR will mean change, for some massive change, much of which is a mind shift. It will affect the organization's strategy, alter responsibilities of staff, require new behaviours, and route out our inefficiencies. Although these types of changes often are used to improve fiscal performance, a CSR program will seek to improve economic, social and environmental performance in a mitigated balance. The campaign for a CSR must start long before the culture of an organization can be affected. There must also be a champion with the power to dream, communicate, and inspire.

At home, employees are leaders in their own right. They make family decisions at the table, include everyone, weigh out the options, persuade each other and make careful consideration in those decisions that may affect all of their lives. Family planning is an ageless tradition that incorporates the dreams, desires and needs of loved ones, looking into the future, balancing risk and reward. Assuming responsibility as head of the household teaches patience, communications skills, and emotional intelligence. Yet, when these same people get to work, a different aura consumes them for the next eight hours. A sociopathy takes place as people divide their dreams from their daily routines and subvert their true desires to perform tasks well below their abilities. That deliberative skill at working towards what is best for the clan is lost because of a much more narrow mandate set by the standards of some manager – that you may not have even met - presides over instinct.

Communications and relations is an area CSR could help expand and enhance. Having a dissonant job is not a true case for everyone, but shouldn't everyone feel devotion and commitment to their work and know they are supported in such a view? Employees will need to be redefining their own jobs which will mean constant but more predictable change. In this way, change is responsibly assumed rather than delegated and a leader needs to orchestrate and point the way.

Implementing a CSR program can create a more innovative company by virtue of the technique of developing a collaborative dynamic and a galvanizing agenda. Building an organic organization begins by understanding our role in the ecosystem. We can co-create a humane workplace where people are valued for their work and what they bring to their work. This requires knowledge management, both intellectual and emotional, and we need to re-define it for business if we are to have the quality of life that the Rosetan community have shown us. The flip side of observing the Rosetan's lifestyle requires us to face that we are currently living in a dysfunctional system that needs attention and action to fix, and thus we need to observe and measure things that we have not even noticed before.

Intelligence is defined as having the abilities, but not limited to, abstract thought, understanding, self-awareness, communication, reasoning, learning, emotional intelligence, memory, planning, and problem solving. Through these abilities we develop talent, awareness and wisdom. Business intelligence is about gathering information and applying knowledge to meet strategic goals, using that information for creating a model of decision-making. Knowledge also lends itself to building and enhancing core competencies that are part of the value of an organization. People are more critical than the plan and a competent and creative force of people must be present in the plan, something of which a good leader will be cognizant.

If the knowledge base of an organization revolves only around profit share and market capture, what will the business do when the community and city officials apply new standards or regulations or new information suggests your business model is now obsolete, especially in terms of environmental change? What happens when there is a talent exodus because company principles and policies are found to not align with changing community and social values that recognize the challenges we face? What will the business do when it comes time to approach its client base and stakeholders about its practices and be truthful? Yes, CSR does include a communications mandate to provide information about progress and community involvement, but more than that it can become a knowledge management tool that enhances the social and environmental sustainability of the organization.

Businesses are becoming less able to predict their true earnings, and corporate corruption has destroyed reputations, family lives and created an industrial legacy that will be passed for generations – not intelligent. In redefining business intelligence, we need to look at the inputs to the organization on a knowledge acquisition level. Using a mind map we can see the various potential inputs to an organizations environmental scan:

Consumers / Competitors / Suppliers / Labour market / Industry / Financial resources — **Organizational Relationships** — Social values / Education / Politics / Legal / Demographics / Natural resources / Technology

Let's look at what Schermerhorn (2008) lists as some of the top trends facing organizations in the new economy:

Belief in human capital: The demands of the new economy require high involvement and work structure that allows for greater participation to contribute knowledge, experience and commitment.

Demise of command and control: Heirarchal structures are too slow, rigid and conservative. Highly interactive network structures allow greater flow of information and resources.

Emphasis on teamwork: Organizations are becoming less vertical and more horizontal in structure as they are more driven by teamwork for creative problem solving.

Pre-eminence of technology: Performing environmental scans can yield new opportunities in technology adoption.

Embrace networking: A networked organization can communicate in real-time and coordinate partners, suppliers and resources more efficiently.

New workforce expectations: The new generation of workforce has less tolerance for hierarchy and formality. Expectations are more for performance-based advancement and less on seniority and status.

Concern for work-life balance: Workers are forcing organization to pay more attention to work—life balance and personal affairs.

Focus on Speed: Products and services are expected to be delivered in a timely manner. Those who can deliver first reap the market advantage.

With these trends in mind, we have to be ahead of the wave in business and building the organization to be leading. Using strategic foresight, we can examine our relationships in the context of future states of environmental and societal being. The trends point to a consciousness raising to reduce the 'toxic workplace' and create more rewarding social networking and an innovative framework – a re-organization. In terms of systems, we need to focus on the relationships we can influence and are influenced by.

Knowledge management is a necessary core competency for performing environmental scans and utilizing strategic foresight. Every organization should have a pro-active scanning strategy to diagnose the complexity and uncertainty in external relationships. Adding the ability to properly manage knowledge assets can stimulate the generation of ideas and innovation, thus generating value and advantage to the company (McLean, 2009), in essence, continuously developing new knowledge.

> *A man does not have himself killed for a half-pence a day or for a petty distinction. You must speak to the soul to electrify him.* - Napolean Bonoparte

Developing new skills and talents in employees does not extend only to adoption of new technologies. The continual threat of obsolescence makes training and retraining necessary for individual growth and organizational success. A successful combination of know-what and know-how will create conditions for good knowledge transfer. Leadership in this context begins to look like a knowledge management worker. As Peter Senge mentioned in his book *The Fifth Discipline,* it is about having the courage to ask 'what do we want to create?' The vision the leader will bring will only ignite people's passion if it is shared with the hearts of others and is inflamed by the leader herself. It is not just about adapting at this point but expanding your ability to create.

Talented workers are knowledge workers whose brains and ideas have become assets for an organization. These people also can see the big picture and have reached higher states of being, thinking, perceiving and emotional intelligence. We all have the ability to be knowledge workers. It is by allowing the abilities to happen through mentorship and learning that creates the capability.

People who have a continuance commitment to the company, those who stay for cash flow purposes only, are not motivated to achieve personal results as they are motivated by other factors. Unfortunately, organizations are not designed to facilitate growing their internal knowledge resources, holding the whole organization back from reaching its potential as a working group. I want to add more to the topic of brain development by emphasizing the importance of nutrition. The physical wellbeing of modern society is in crisis and also needs reorganization. The barrage of cheap fast foods and pesticide-laden imports have polluted our bodies and lands. This topic is another book! But please join me and acknowledge that we can learn all we want, but without the proper physical well being, nutrition and balance we will not grow into a fundamentally civilised race.

A balanced approach takes into account the non-monetary factors that support the strategy and economic success of a business. This means considering and integrating social and environmental considerations and opportunities into the operation, promotions and delivery of business. Sometimes the considerations are called the 'triple bottom line' or the three-legged stool. These misnomers have a tendency to merge priorities rather than develop a specific core competency for social responsibility. An example is the idea that not using plastic bags will save the environment. This helps, but stops short of examining participating business operations, the work cultures involved, the supply-chains and public relations that could decrease costs, engage community and lower impacts on air, water and nature. It's not about the bags at all, rather the ethic of displacing harmful activity. An organization that pursues knowledge management in social and environmental practice is also more savvy to resource sensitivities, more dynamic and flexible to changes in economy, and reduces risk and exposure to forthcoming legislation and operating requirements.

The new values in an organization will see business and society as interrelated not in opposition. As Michael Porter and Mark Kramer put it:

"The prevailing approaches to CSR are so disconnected from business as to obscure many of the greatest opportunities for companies to benefit society." (Porter & Kramer, 2006)

The world is moving from a competitive individualistic prerogative to a socialistic mutually rewarding and necessary collaborative venture to improve business and life – proving economy and environment are not mutually exclusive. The diversity of companies and talent is an advantage to any organization that knows how to engage and create synergy within new networks. New and diverse perspectives must be nurtured and rewarded in a positive manner to facilitate idea generation and inspiration. A good CSR program will incorporate this approach to program development.

The new organizational consciousness is about a shift in perception and core beliefs. People once believed that leaded makeup was fine because it had no perceivable immediate impacts on health. Today lead has supposedly been eliminated as a gasoline additive and a makeup enhancer because science has acquired the knowledge and shared it to a great extent, yet it remains – incredibly - in such items as children's toys, the last place you would expect to look. And, cigarettes used to be campaigned as endorsed by doctors. The costs of these beliefs are unsurmountable, still have effects today, and will for a long-time. These are the same long-term costs that must be understood in strategic planning. We must ask what beliefs are we holding today that are keeping us from a brighter healthier future.

We verify impacts through rigor and science, prove the relationship, establish knowledge through discovery of truth and adopt it as a core belief so that we may behave accordingly to our best interests of health and security. One may notice this is in stark contrast to current politics. Politicians bend and sway to people's opinion to renew their position in power, never committing to long-term progress or using science to make compelling arguments. Government has become a bulky slow and immutable bureaucracy, perhaps good for doing things right but not necessarily doing the right things. Business operates with more dynamic and flexibility. It has the ability to move with the times and lead the way provided the vision and determination are there.

Moving In A New Direction

In moving past old beliefs, the new consciousness is also an integrated approach to the various systems that our institutions interact with. In the case of urbanization, most of us are well aware of the impacts of poorly designed development. Suburban sprawl has destroyed watersheds and valuable farmland and designed a system that limits improvements in transportation, reforestation, waste management and community involvement. We are now re-thinking the way we develop, even to the point where we are questioning growth itself. Our core values desire the right information to move towards healthy, happy lives and re-establish the strength of community and regionalism. A societal responsibility initiative is happening as we speak.

The next illustration is an example of how Hawken and Lovins' depict the type of thinking around economy and where we should be:

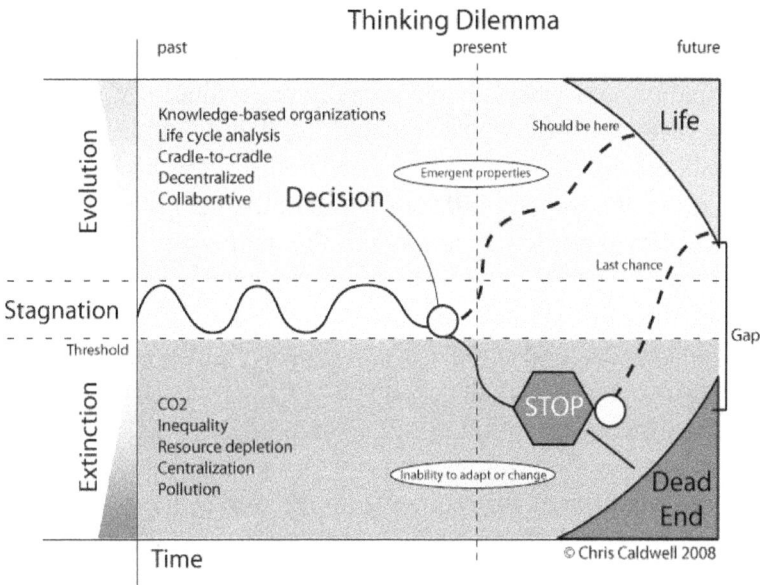

Thinking Dilemma

This image was made to communicate graphically the need to understand our direction of thinking and change course in methods of decision making. I examined previous decisions made and provided decision support for current projects and offered recommendations for improving their processes. As the illustration shows, poor decisions in the past have led to a decline in systems over time. This could be economic, social or environmental. If we do not stop proceeding along the path that a poor decision has initiated then we can, of course, predict further decline. But time is of the essence. The STOP symbol represents the point of no return and marks the gap we have to make up to reach objectives required by larger order systems.

It is the size of the gap of that determines the margin by which we can manoeuvre to turn things around – otherwise known as performance gap management. The most critical and complex variable is in this graph is the consideration of time. We do not know how much time we have because of a lack of information about our impacts on those higher order systems. To use a metaphor, it is as if the human race is in a giant Sports Utility Vehicle headed for a cliff. Everyone on board is fussing and trying their damnedest to make it more efficient and eco-friendly instead of putting the brakes on and turning it around.

When we determine an attractive authentic vision of where we need and want to go, we attract others to the cause. People naturally want to be a part of something positive and socially rewarding, if not historically significant. This is also the mark of leading organizations – that they embrace change and with it, new forms of thinking and perceiving that create innovation through ingenuity, lasting change. A more ecological based approach, not just in the natural sense but in terms of integrating systems, allows for reducing or at least gaining a better understanding of the uncertainty and complexity of problem-solving. CSR is not just a do-good feel-good project, it is a scientific and moral assertion that brings the organization out of the dark and asserts a more inventive direction.

In an eco-systems approach, all problems are seen as systems based and approached as such. For example, environmental management is sometimes constricted to visible problems, such as the impact of urbanization. The interaction of human social systems and environment has a host of complex relationships that unless understood together, result in new problems to both systems. Appreciating that humans are actually creatures of the ecological system first and foremost, an intersection of socio-eco systems for problem solving makes more sense if we are to have a realistic model for a sustainable future. Our understanding of systems are only as good as the models we develop to represent our ideas. We often forget that we are observing from the inside out, being a part of the system, rather than observing from the outside-in, like a petri dish under a microscope. It is quite easy to rely on our senses alone and miss feedback and information that will allow us to make better decisions.

Humans also have a penchant to look for ready answers or a universal solution that explains a condition, that once found becomes the overarching policy. While convenient for examining large populations in stable conditions, this is poor for working with complex and dynamic systems. Our ability to produce adaptive and resilient responses to changes in our environment is drastically reduced.

By introducing an interdisciplinary stakeholder approach we can reduce the mono-culture of the mind by pooling our perceptions. Decisions become less expert-driven and more expertly collaborative. It is in adaptive management that we will find the future of business and society in responding to global challenges. The last thing we want is for decisions concerning the environment to be left to a small group of people who dissect it as a problem rather than treating it as our mutual home and realize we all share a part in its stewardship.

Systems Thinking

In times of change, the learners will inherit the earth, while the learned find themselves beautifully equipped with a world that no longer exists – Eric Hoffer

Systems thinking is literally thinking and seeing in systems with your mind's eye. It involves greater consideration and inspection of what on the surface appears to be a singular and consistent event, which upon deeper investigation yields supporting and nurturing relationships. When we talk of ecosystems, organizations and communities we are talking in terms of systems. Systems processes reveal a complex series of interactions, all of which are inter-related. When people think of systems many think of technology. Certainly systems hardware and software play a role in the way we think of how to apply a solution to a problem. Information systems help us organize mountains of data and find anomalies. What I am referring to is systems philosophy – a reorientation of a world view as a new scientific paradigm. It extends beyond how we look at a problem to how we see ourselves and our roles within the problem and solution: a perfect beginning to a CSR program. In a systems perspective, we look at the interaction between knower and known which is dependent on a number of factors of a biological, cultural, psychological, linguistic, etc., nature (Bertalanffy & Laszlo, 1972).

Decisions based on seeing a single element of a system neglects the system as a whole, making the decision essentially meaningless in the long-term as the implications of pursuing a course of action based on poor information will degrade that same system. This is eveident in our policies and continued degradation. We have unfortunately developed a culture of analytical thinking or rational planning, one that breaks elements down, reducing them to simpler elements, which constricts scope and consideration. For example, the fisheries have long been a source of food and economy. Bountiful harvests of fish appear to be never ending cascade and source of energy but we know from more science and application that it is much more complex than that and in fact, we are depleting the system of its entities. Our current way of thinking of operating, planning and management does not work and requires a change in understanding, scope and approach.

Modern science and business analytics use methods of reductionism to develop a mental concept and make decisions for progress. The problem with reductionism is that it compartmentalizes and decomposes a system into minute details that can only appear as linear elements because the scope is empiric and not holistic. The mental models, as a result, are reinforced even in the face of imminent collapse. Routines in thought and practice end up analysing attributes of elements and not the behaviour of the system within which our organizations depend. The holism of thought creates greater understanding by acknowledging the relationships between elements and their recursive properties with other elements and to the system as a whole. Only by examining relationships within a system can patterns emerge that lead to greater understanding.

Systems build resilience by reinforcing and creating new elements or entities. New entities mean a greater possibility for relationships and interaction among other entities in the system. These entities co-evolve and create new emergent properties - something new emerges from the system of which it was not previously capable. The diversity of the system increases and so does the complexity. They go hand in hand.

In human organizations (which are systems), allowing a critical rate of elements to develop and interact and evolve into a network model should, in theory, generate an explosion of creativity and innovation as well as diversity and complexity complementary to innovation. New entities in the system, whether technological, virtual teams, or other forms of social organization, can create new niches. This type

71

of evolution explains the difference between highly adaptive societies able to create innovation and those that fail and are left behind (Homer-Dixon, 2000).

Most consider complexity an enemy of organization, when in fact it is just an attribute of greater sophistication. Thus, simplifying something to make it more convenient may erase a complex system or opportunity that has capabilities to deal with increased pressures of competition or stress. Eventually, newly created systems increase in complexity to become naturally resilient and task lower order systems to support its own growth. Once we used electrons only to light bulbs, now we hold them in certain sequences for programmable software and holding information in a computerized format. Things only evolve when a new relationship is discovered and there are a multitude of relationships humans have with economic, social and environmental systems that are yet to be explored.

Complexity is a key element of why systems thinking needs to be a part of every policy decision, especially in sustainable development or in programs such a social responsibility. It makes sense to merge social and environmental systems when developing or improving a CSR-related project or program or to tackle growing environmental issues. Complexity's twin is diversity. Reducing problems so that decisions are made more readily omits all the knowledge and information available from utilizing a systems perspective.

Classical management theory and techniques are becoming less applicable in the face of greater complexity. Current management mainly works on static models and ideal volatility conditions, creating the perception of an environment of certainty in which to do business. The recent sub-prime mortgage crisis revealed the flaws of false predictability and highlighted the need for reform in ethics and approach to managing business. The reduction of business planning to pure economic indicators for quick productive turnover, will in the end, result in greater costs and once again, reactive rather than adaptive planning. Leaders will attempt to reduce uncertainty by focusing on what it is they do know and can control. "Such prediction and control is unlikely to be possible in the future and unless expectations on leaders change, the conflict between the desire for certainty and the reality of uncertainty will result in leaders who are unable to manage in an uncertain world (Davis & Blass, 2007, p. 41)."

Most managers derive their decision-making models from within the system in which they operate, seeing the inputs, throughputs and outputs. Systemic flaws are not revealed until a crisis occurs and then it becomes a reaction rather than a plan. The subjective view of the organization and externalization of the interrelationships, economic, social and environmental, creates a false paradigm of thinking and knowledge. We are still managing as if we are in a closed system. For an adaptive CSR program to take hold, consider illustrating the processes and cycles of inputs and outputs and using them to better see the relationships between elements in the systems. Systems thinking is difficult for most people but can be learned like anything. Empirical research suggests that current executives and managers are not systems or post-conventional thinkers even though understanding the dynamics of a system is imperative (Waddock & McIntosh, 2009).

Systems thinking is not about reconstructing our civilization or rewiring our brains, rather it is about taking a unique perspective that will change the approach to planning and evaluating programs, policies and initiatives (Cabrera, Colosi, & Lobdell, 2008, p. 300). This may also mean abandoning the familiar 'strategic planning' approach that dominates today. Strategies are generally left to experts or people in power, creating a vision that may be prone to cultural imperialism.

An adaptive management process must take place, one that adjusts to knowledge gathered by the organization. Waldman (2007) suggest two reasons why strategic planning will not work: 1) the system is composed of people who must be engaged and take ownership to create change, otherwise they will subvert to the status quo; and 2) the self-organizing system will reject human intervention if it does not align with the structure and function of the natural system.

Human nature will have to give up control of planning to forces of nature simply because humans never had control in the first place.

73

One such example is hurricane Katrina and the aftermath. Should homes and businesses be rebuilt using contemporary planning standards or should the area be naturalized and new innovation brought in? Will people plan with hurricanes and natural systems in mind and innovate new buildings, streamlined and water safe that provide shelter in such circumstances or build standard design infrastructure with no resilience? Systems thinking can also establish resilience by aligning planning and human systems with natural systems, developing harmony rather than interference with the interrelationships.

Using systems thinking, we respect the political and natural boundaries to which we are applying our plans. Systems analysis and focus require a boundary to distinguish it from its environment for two reasons: 1) all systems are interrelating with the environment at all times, exchanging energy and matter and; 2) the human mind and technology cannot reduce the complexity of systems to a workable scale unless a boundary is established.

System structure or organizational structure determines the dynamics or behaviour of a system. The behaviour of a system displays emergent properties that cannot be reconstructed from the individual elements; the whole is literally greater than the sum of the parts. Behaviour is not always or simultaneously displayed as some elements cycle in relationships in different temporal scales, moving in biorhythmic oscillations. In other words, systems are non-linear. This may be a hard concept to grasp but the dynamics in a system are not something that can be statistically interpolated and predicted as such. It would be like trying to determine the weather in a long range forecast.

The less we understand how elements in a system relate, the less we can predict the outcomes of tweaking system elements. Experimentation is a method of learning and should be encouraged, however, when we know that a system is degrading because of our experiment, we should cease activity lest we eliminate the system altogether. The Precautionary Principle is based on this premise.

In summary, systems thinking requires concepts of holism, relationships, boundaries, feedback, organization, time delays, and emergence (Abou-Zeid, 2008, pp. 11-12). Applying systems thinking to perform systems analysis focuses on the interactions and impacts of human activities. To understand those interactions, the type and integrity of information for analysis is important. The immediate advantage to decision making comes in the form of performing strategic foresight or modelling once relationships between elements become clear. But there are limitations.

It is not possible to predict the future with any given accuracy. Investments always depend on future developments, such as energy pricing, and thus uncertainty is one element of decision-making that must always exist as a factor. This is the essence of the precautionary principal that dictates that no decisions should be made if you cannot reduce or eliminate the harm that may occur as a result of its implementation. Some governments and businesses have enacted Environmental Assessments which gathers more rigorous information that may modify or even eliminate the project. Infrastructure is one such example. In past, building a highway was a matter of finding the money and levelling the ground. Now, we may be destroying a sensitive habitat for a rare species or disturbing a watershed that could flood hundreds of homes down water. These things we only know because we went deeper into the relationships to look at the systems involved.

Existing knowledge bases, such as chemical impacts or environmental sensitivities do not cover concise artefacts of information that may be needed to make a more informed decision. Building a good knowledge base about your business and the impacts of your activities is the first place to start. Information systems, worker engagement, best practice and legacy can assist in determining where those impacts exist and can be addressed.

Technologies used for performing analysis can only provide quality data at the time of their use. Data captured ten years ago with older technology and possibly out-dated techniques may not be robust enough to be used for future prediction. Science is constantly changing and systems are dynamic. Therefore examining and establishing new information gathering techniques is a dynamic and necessary function of the new organization. For example, a company may invest in real-time monitoring to mange anything from logistic to water use.

In applying boundaries, we usually consider space but often not time. Measurements or assessments done in the present may inform our current decision process but how does that inform us on how future indicators such as pollution or emissions are to be valued against our present assessment? Future impacts are not less important as today's. We cannot discount social and environmental factors the same as we practice economic discounting. The use of a variety of indicators and information-gathering techniques requires appropriate weighing and prioritization. This may be the best time to initiate a discussion and include stakeholder input for determining critical factors for analysis. Look at the social systems linked to the organization through the employees and surrounding communities.

Develop your own system scope versus the geographic or political boundaries. Emissions and human impacts do not have human-centric boundaries and so when determining the scope for setting the project or analysis, anything 'downwind' or 'downriver' must be included. Engage stakeholders for traditional or practical knowledge on new topics. Best practice research will save a lot of time and effort instead of re-inventing the wheel.

In a systems approach, the whole is greater than the sum of the parts. Emergent properties are attributes in a system that form when new relationships are created and stabilized. These are capabilities that manifest when a synergy is created in a group that no individual could achieve on their own. This is why divisiveness is destructive – it negates potential and makes systems less resilient. Just as in chemistry and mixing the right amounts can produce something new or destructive, the same needs to occur in organizations. Understand your environmental relationships and people relationships to reveal emergent properties.

The strength of your organization lies in the diversity of properties and functions within the systems. These are not functions that can be teased out but have to be nurtured. Talent, observation, and consideration along with knowledge management will allow new capabilities. Opportunities are only restricted by the scope of view. If there are not enough options, create some.

Sustainable Change Management

The traditional perception of CSR is a strategic over-arching change to the organization resulting in greater social investment for the benefit of company and community. The view of CSR as a strategy, automatically suggests a top-down management approach is required to achieve objectives, but change can be instituted from the lower levels as a strategic incremental plan thus including employees in the process. Getting buy-in from the formal and informal parts of the organization is not difficult if the initiatives represent the values of the employees and reflect real-world needs.

Approaches to CSR are steeped in classical management theory and administrative science. This is because boards are still unsure if instituting a CSR program is financially viable and thus are hesitant to release control of old methods of developing a business case; they equate it to an advertising campaign or research initiative that has no immediate financial return. The framing of CSR as a business case keeps the development of a CSR strategy a responsibility of upper management when, in actuality, the nature of a CSR program is to increase inclusivity of employees and community that reaps both social and economic benefits.

The benefits in a participatory employee-centred approach include better adaptability in dynamic and uncertain environments. As we enter more volatile economic, societal, and environmental conditions, an organization that is best suited for continuous change will flourish. Walter Nord and Sally Fuller (Nord & Fuller, 2009) examined organizational change and increasing CSR adoption and contrasted the limitations of a traditional top-down approach with an employee-centred approach. This is not to say a top-down approach is not good. Interface Flooring commanded reductions in material use and chemicals that both saved money, raised image, increased innovation

77

and lowered the environmental footprint of the company. Nord and Fuller are examining the limitations that could occur as a result of employing a top-down approach in CSR.

Employees that receive generous business intelligence and are given authority to act on their responsibilities will display emergent properties for the organization. These properties are something that cannot be accounted for by any strategic plan but contribute greatly to the resilience and robustness of the organization. An organization is the sum of its relationships.

Emergent properties surface during change through centralization to decentralization, from static order to dynamic, and by redistributing power and decision-making.

However, hierarchy may be deeply ingrained and so change can be disorienting, even fearful. It may be best to develop an incremental plan for engaging stakeholders and achieving objectives. Work out the little milestones and celebrate those successes along the way. When initiating the change, it is important to let people know why the change is happening, what the benefits are and why they should agree.

Decentralizing for the sake of decentralizing can cost a lot of time and money, there needs to be set objectives in re-organizing. Rob Cross et al. (Cross, 2009), examined the role of informal networks in decision making. They found in their research that engineers and scientists were roughly five times as likely to go to a friend or colleague for information to assist in decision making than to repositories of knowledge; literally enacting the 'it's who you know' notion. This can also work in reverse, facilitating network resistance to decisions already made.

Leaders may recognize systems and networks but fail to leverage them properly. Decision making can be hampered by not getting the right people involved and by too much collaboration. Sixty per cent of the time employees used to make decisions was with networking with peers that were not involved in the actual decision making (ibid, 36). Failure to define roles and responsibilities can devolve decision making and empower others, creating bottlenecks, costing more time and money.

Cross et al listed three initiatives in one of their study organizations of 3000 people within the pharmaceutical industry, that reduce the 'cross-talk' and increase decision effectiveness:

- Fewer interactions – reduce the number of steps and people involved. Simplify the decision stream by clearly delegating roles and responsibilities

- Fewer and smaller committees – reduce the number and size of committees, streamline meetings and develop guideline on decision making rights

- Revised leadership training – included conflict resolution training, decision making proficiency became a necessary core competency and greater accountability in demonstrating the meeting of their assigned roles and less interference in non-routine decisions

- Improving the top team decision making was possible because of the information gathering done, examining and mapping the network and processes of the organization

"Top teams are the core of decision making in critical processes such as strategic planning, resource allocation and conflict resolution — activities that have direct and indirect impacts on organizations. Yet too often efforts to improve decision making focus on symptoms — for example, engaging in team building to enhance collaboration when the underlying problem is something else" (Cross, 2009, p. 39).

Small wins are the achievements of individuals and teams in the organizations that contribute to the over all objectives and vision. By redistributing organizational intelligence (information and decision-making), the company increases its chances of achieving 'small wins' and thus increasing the odds of future success in projects by creating a culture of achievement.

Nord and Fuller recommend several steps to engage the employee-centred approach:

> First, provide training to introduce supervisor and lower level participants to the small wins notion and related ideas from Weick (1984) and Meyerson and Scully (1995).

> Second, educate all employees to the idea that some of the organization's CSR progress depends on grass-roots initiatives from lower-level participants.

> Third, encourage supervisors to make note of, reward and otherwise foster lower-level CSR initiatives.

> Fourth, consider taking advantage of the electronic technology prominent in today's organizations by offering, for example, a Grassroots CSR Wiki...These actions could include making employee-centred CSR potential a criterion in hiring as well as developing a strong organizational culture supportive of CSR and employee involvement (Nord & Fuller, 2009, p. 289).

Greater employee involvement in the CSR program development can also develop trust and organizational citizenship behaviours.

Job design is an important factor of any small or large organization. People care about the tasks assigned to them, the interdependency of those tasks with others and the influence of their work to perform positive metaphysical changes in their environment. Scientific management of the past has stressed the division of labour for production efficiency, which works well in theory. However, work simplification can have the effect of dumbing down a work force and creating work alienation.

The search for meaningfulness in one's job is paramount for motivation and to excel and move toward the self-actualized roles of leader and teacher. There is even a notion of 'workplace spirituality' which is distinguished by creating an interconnectedness among staff and dispelling negativity, excessive control, egocentric behaviour, mistrust, dishonesty, back-stabbing, and a strong hierarchy (Sniderman & Nelson, 2007, p. 125).

The CSR program brings this meaningfulness to the organization as it illuminates the connections from one's work to higher order systems of the organization, community and the environment. Indeed, it can become the core motivator and source of pride for all stakeholders.

Make Change The New Standard

Many companies have a social and environmental system or committee that looks to see what the management of the company can do to become more socially responsible. Often though, these systems are not integrated into the general management of the firm and so the links and contributions to community and the environment remain unclear, as does the role of the committee or manager in developing high-performance work practices (HPWP). Even when the links are more clear as in the cases of obtaining certification in SA8000, ISO 14000 and FLA, the endless amount of forms, rules, and multiple visits from external compliance auditors can blur identifying what standards or internal factors are valid measures of true social responsibility. These codes and standards might be preferred or required by clients, but managers are often inundated with surveys regarding their ethical policies and understanding the values internal to the organization. There is also no agreement on what environmental performance is and how to measure it.

Those companies instituting environmental management systems (EMS) such as ISO 14001, have differing priorities as to the objectives of the EMS. The performance of such systems varies according to such intangibles as corporate culture, values and competitive environment. A business survey of EMS highlighted fourteen benefits as strengthening innovation, customer loyalty, safeguarding against legislation, enhancing corporate image. Only three identified benefits actually related to environmental performance and impact. It is difficult to examine the usefulness of such systems when voluntary mechanisms do not require public disclosure. This also limits benchmarking with similar businesses. The effectiveness of an EMS appears to rely heavily on other factors

81

such as management style, goals and mission, operating environment, culture and stakeholders (Nawrocka & Parker, 2009).

Standards can be a good idea at first but become a bad idea later. Changing environmental and resource conditions can obliterate standards, which can lead to quick obsolescence in an economic or ecological crisis. An adaptive management approach is best suited for planning around complex and diverse issues. Develop your team and organization in an adaptive environment, one that supports insight, ideas, and change.

In determining the sustainability of a company, a CSR program is but one step in recognizing resource constraints, the impact of corporate culture and the links between mental and physical health of employees and business performance. Sustainable business may be interpreted as being able to continue business in harsher climates by shifting resources or having labour increase production under limited budget, both of which can have short-term gain but long-term disastrous effects. For a business to be sustainable it must remain competitive and develop a collaborative approach, especially when environmental factors will become a larger determinant of the success of that business.

Organizational Culture

Organizational effectiveness is the primary driver for leadership and vice versa. There are two perspectives on leadership and effectiveness. The first defines effectiveness as an organization that consistently achieves its goals. The second, and more applicable to the changing times is, an organization that acquires and develops its core competencies and capacity (Andreadis, 2009). The latter framework positions an organization to realize greater possibilities because the driving force is progress and thus greater capability.

Operations and infrastructure are still being deployed with the conventional management approaches that require predictability and closed organizational boundaries. Globalization, technology, and social and cultural diversity are changing the face of business and communications. Waddock and McIntosh (2009) highlight the attributes of business in the new economy. Businesses need to be:

Networked and interdependent – the organization does not exist independent and separate from other organizations and the environment. It must be integrative with government, education, civil society and communities. The business must also develop models of collaboration and understand the health of a related system affects the health of the organization.

Flexible and adaptive – a slow-moving bureaucracy is likely to be unsuccessful in a chaotic and changing world. Nimble and adaptive managers will find more opportunities and must be open to revisiting scale and scope of business interests. As the economic crisis has shown, large and powerful businesses are prone to fail because of regimented and out-dated practices.

Relational and equitable – to create the connectivity with stakeholders, fair representation of those involved is necessary to build relationships that sustain. The ability to see and be empathic to the diversity of interests will reward in hard times.

Demanding shared power – expanding the knowledge economy means including others in the decision making process and thus altering the power structure. This also creates alliances of shared intellectual wealth.

Leaderful – New forms of leadership need to be nurtured and assigned. The servant-leader will become the leader of preference for an organization, demonstrating the entrepreneurial spirit and capability to develop talent to drive success at all levels. "Leaderfulness, as defined by Raelin, is not heroic, top down, autocratic, or demanding of others, but shared across levels, initiated anywhere, and comes from anyone with insights, ideas, and knowledge that inspire others with a sense of purpose and meaning (Waddock & McIntosh, 2009, p. 303)."

Fulfilling the above five points requires shifting the purpose of the firm. Challenges of climate change, economic crisis, unstable

83

economies and social institutions and volatility means corporations must go back to their roots of serving the public interest. By taking a systems approach to organizational effectiveness, we can build organizations that are meant to last. In other words, leaders cannot rely on good luck or timing, they must institute elements of competence, adaptability, and commit to integrating learning into strategy, processes and behaviours that will allow the organization to remain sustainable despite turbulence in its environment (Andreadis, 2009).

A sustainable organization can also be described as one whose characteristics and actions are designed to lead to a "desirable future state" for all stakeholders (Funk, 2003). The manager of an organization is key to creating the high performance synergy among their workers by supporting and encouraging the wise use of talent and resources. This makes the manager a key player in social responsibility and sustainable development of the business.

Businesses and organizations physically structure themselves dependent on the business processes that require fulfilling. A high degree of command and control dictates a sharp pyramidal shape while an entrepreneurial organization necessitates a flattened network structure. The shape of an organization has a direct influence on the communications ability, and thus on the innovation and sociality of its members. An authoritarian, bureaucratic or militaristic shape is pointed with a high degree of hierarchy, much like a pyramid while a flatter and more rounded organization is more characteristic of free agency or entrepreneurial networking.

To invoke the creativity and spirit of workers, employees or group members, the degree of separation must be lessened. A centralized structure has a way of compartmentalizing information and thus producing a separation not necessarily in body, but in mind and spirit. When communication is stifled, it creates disparate work conditions.

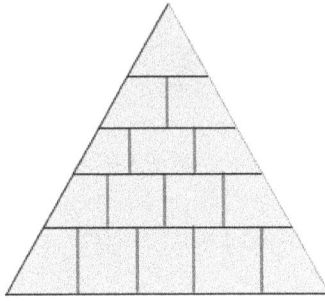

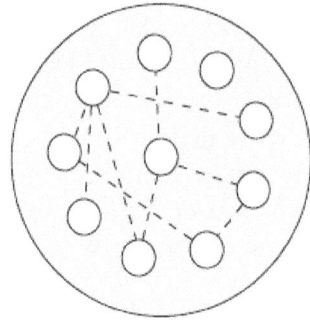

CENTRALIZED   DE-CENTRALIZED

To highlight the difference that density and cohesiveness has on prompting innovation, an interesting study was done on the difference in urban form and innovation. The fundamental idea of radical innovation and group acceptance applies to planners and their work with communities as well. Sosa and Gero presented results from a study of innovation through computational social simulations. Their work focused on the degrees of separation and how it affected the spread of ideas. This has a parallel with density of population and innovation considerations for planners.

To spread ideas and solutions to replace existing widespread practices in society, the planner must understand how ideas are adopted and disseminated. Sosa and Gero's models found that high degrees of separation (such as those found in suburbs) resisted the flow of new ideas but were fertile ground for individual alternative ideas to be attempted. However, influence is more at a regional level. Societies where more strangers exist, are more open to social change (such as cities). Societies that were more acquainted with each other are more likely to reinforce existing ideas, habits and customs (Sosa & Gero, 2008), but once an idea takes hold it spreads more quickly. These ideas might be more clear if we summarize them as a social transmission of behaviour.

We can see the implications for innovation in ensuring that a supporting structure with an appropriate density that generates and incubates ideas is properly organized. If an organization is structured properly, it may generate its own ideas and innovation, facilitating knowledge worker growth and contribution and be balanced enough in delegation and autonomy that innovation may spread spontaneously with greater effectiveness. The key here is network cohesion.

It is especially important for young firms to expand their network to access intellectual and financial resources. The development stages that characterize start-ups and innovators require new actors to be drawn and sometimes recruited to stimulate efforts. Building those new relationships, including customers, will mean risking change and losing existing relationships and even changing the conditions and characteristics of the firm itself (Oberg & Grundstrom, 2009). By engaging new network contacts, obligations or power struggles could arise unless clearly defined roles are communicated.

Management Psyche

The link between structure and behaviour becomes clear when we bring psychology into the picture. Large organizations become more representative of the society of origin in their geography of work. Thus a cross section of population from the workplace will look more and more like the regional communities as it grows, unless purposely skewed by stringent requirements such as specific work skills or discriminating in hiring practices. There are cases where global organizations enforce their corporate culture on the communities and thus the population puts on a 'blue suit' in order to obtain the status and employment within the organization.

The skewing or hiring can be culturally biased. Many organizations have a self-fulfilling prophesy in that although they may want to change and hire creative types they could fall into hiring analytical types only or hire what they know and are familiar with because it is comfortable. Status quo persists and whatever creative disruption exists becomes isolated. The people performing critical thinking may become depressed and leave. Change management would be difficult indeed if the narcissism in management reinforced itself by hiring the image in the mirror.

Small organisations are typically centred on values and mission, from the entrepreneur with a vision and motivation to a start-up group seeking to succeed on their own. Small scale groups have a different dynamic. People in small groups wear many hats and are driven by goals rather than monetary gain. Large groups have much to learn from small groups. In fact, as Richard Branson suggests and has put into practice, any department that becomes too big is disbanded and managed as smaller groups to maintain a critical edge.

Malcolm Gladwell reveals in his book *The Tipping Point*, just how small groups can be more influential in spreading a new idea. It requires that different types of people (connectors, mavens and salesman) need to promote the idea and the idea has to be 'sticky' in that it sustains attention. The context or environment in which the idea spreads is important to allow the idea to tip into popularity. Thus organizations would benefit from a decentralized, networked, small group structure if they seek innovation and resilience in a changing environment.

Gladwell shows that groups of certain sizes and certain types can often be uniquely conducive to achieving the tipping point. He examines the popularity of the book *The Divine Secrets of the Ya-Ya Sisterhood* from regional following to national best-seller. The unique content appealed strongly to reading groups of middle-aged women in Northern California, who were uniquely positioned to catapult the book to national success as a result of informal campaigning.

Gladwell reinforces the unusual properties of smaller groups. Groups of less than 150 members usually display a level of intimacy, interdependency, and efficiency that begins to dissipate as soon as the group's size increases beyond 150. This concept has been exploited by a number of corporations that use it as the foundation of their organizational structures and marketing campaigns.

This is why government and corporations find themselves in 'groupthink' or with bad management practices. In a society where narcissism is prevalent, managers with self-image problems or self-serving agendas cannot function objectively for the best needs of their team, project or community; they just do not have the skills. Many core competencies, alternatives and opportunities are overlooked as a result. The image the manager portrays is unauthentic and in a

87

narcissistic personality type, is typically opposite to the individual true self. For example, a manager may compensate by overseeing the work of others through a command and conquer attitude, yet feels helpless in his own life to create the changes necessary to be happy. We often project unto others the very flaws we fail to see in our selves.

Narcissism in society can reveal itself in many ways in the organization, but primarily in insecurity. Individuals wield a self-image that is acceptable to the group or corporate culture and may not be in conflict with their true self or inner values. This stress in behaviour leads to dissonance and a lack of authenticity. Playing dual roles in life is unauthentic. However, it is important to differentiate between psychological narcissism and adopting culture to fit in. For example, the profession of international trade requires learning cultural idioms and customs to refrain from insulting other cultures and to ensure good relations.

Underlying all of our roles in life at work and at home is our psychological makeup. Managers of the future, much like marketers will be fluent in psychology, understanding group dynamics and individual behaviour. This is not something that is left to human resources, a department that has been relegated to ensuring the smooth flow of benefits, insurance and replacing turnover. Rather a 'pre-active' approach is needed for managers. When managers are schooled in behaviour and people's psyche long before taking on a role that requires supervision of others, things change for the better. Having a manager that is supportive, understanding and non-narcissistic is a big incentive for people to perform and stay long term.

Companies strive to find the right reward incentive mix to attract, motivate and retain talent. Employees are expected to commit to become high performers, but if the structure and incentives do not appeal, they may never reach their potential while on the job. The worst case is to have high employee turnover.

Appealing to the value system of employees will encourage their involvement and contribution to organizational knowledge. An organization's ability to leverage existing knowledge as well as generate new knowledge is the currency for success and the source of sustained competitive advantage (Guidice, Heames, & Wang, 2009, p. 143).

Developing potential is becoming an increasingly important part of modern living, as community and world issues demand we act. People want to allow the goodness in them to operate and to heed the call of good citizenship, to reach their higher selves and express through their individual strengths. The need to develop talent is the driving force for many people and is key to achieving life satisfaction. Fear can hold people back from becoming their best.

The feeling of great self-worth is invaluable in a world where distractions are manufactured to keep us from thinking too much about who we are and what we are meant to do. We settle for the mundane, allow negativity to creep into our lives, and allow the influence of others to manipulate for self-interest, all of which comes full circle to the organization or community, creating a toxic environment. We have all experienced this. An organization that can provide the environment to allow individuals to self-actualize and flourish will have built a family of employees and an internal community that will go the extra mile to ensure the organization's security and higher order needs.

We must have an understanding of what drives commitment and motivation in individuals to begin to develop something applicable as a management and CSR tool. Psychology, anthropology, and social studies can shed light on the human psyche, culture and group behaviour and thus how corporate citizenship behaviour can be increased.

Systems thinking, creative direction and engagement will create the space for new ideas. Ideas based on improving the organization and community are usually selfless, appeal to progress, and may be health oriented. At the same time they are genuine in offering assistance to enhance the business profile, so they should be heard and discussed if proposed with integrity. Typically, responsible or ethical behaviour is not rewarded or even noticed in an organization. It can be hard to

89

establish a positive work culture or institute a values-driven workplace without this support and recognition.

Management typically relies on technology and policy to undertake management initiatives, ignoring the huge potential to engage their own employees that are already poised to act from their own value positions. These behaviours can be further defined as "individual behaviour that is discretionary, not directly or explicitly recognized by the formal reward system, and in the aggregate promotes the efficient and effective functioning of the organization." (Organ, Podsakoff, & MacKenzie, 2006).

Aligning values of the corporation with the values of the community results in many benefits. Management knows the importance of cooperation between employees, employee activity outside of the basic job description, knowledge sharing, pro-social behaviours and personal development. The pro-social behaviours extend into different themes of helping (proactive collaboration), sportsmanship (taking on challenges with others), organizational loyalty (defending the mission and brand), organizational compliance (respect for policies and rules) and self-development (individual initiative and the seeking of knowledge that benefits both the individual and organization). (Boiral, 2009, p. 223).

There is difficulty in recognizing pro-social and pro-environmental behaviour because of the often anonymous and ambiguous nature of the activities. Reward and incentive systems fail to recognize the intangibles and value that knowledge workers bring. Reinforcing those behaviours that utilize employee talents for the good of organization and community will keep everyone happy.

We previously looked at the consumer ethic and its impacts on attitudes and values. We have also seen how being stuck in that ethic can keep an individual from attaining higher order satisfaction related more to relationships, wisdom, and achievement. While Maslow's Hierarchy is just a theory, it has been useful in developing further theories and practice in organizational behaviour to understand motivation and reward incentives, and the role they play in organizational excellence.

McClelland's theory of learned needs suggests that human needs are not hierarchal, and are learned rather than innate. The theory centres on an individual's need for achievement, power and affiliation. Entrepreneurs rank highly in the need for achievement and want feedback on their work efforts. The need for power can be personal or social. The social side is concerned about influencing others for the greater good, while the personal need for power can be destructive.

Finally, the need for affiliation requires good cohesive relationships and harmony. McClelland's theories are more closely related to an organizational CSR program and applying this theory can facilitate needs in employees who are entrepreneurial minded. Going beyond the standard definitions of CSR must include fulfilling higher order employee needs by allowing personal and professional growth. By reinforcing behaviours that align with corporate objectives that also include employee's personal values, the organization will self-organize through sheer motivation.

Building value through social capital

> *"It is not the strongest that survive, but those most adaptive to change." – Charles Darwin*

We are trained from a young age that resources are limited and that we must compete for them: that the strongest survive. Many games as youngsters often portray being the solitary winner of a group or being the best by outwitting or outperforming your cohorts. We can see that this mentality pervades economic competition today. The time and resources spent just competing could be used to accomplish more together than we ever could individually. We must question, in a world with limited resources and growing social and environmental issues, 'what does it mean to win?'

Cities spend a great deal of money trying to lure business in the globalized economy, yet that is somehow counter-intuitive to fostering talent and developing business and capacity within the local community and city itself. If we are to truly be sustainable we must either find free clean energy to perform global trade and commerce, or develop regional self-sustaining economies that provide employment and local manufacture. From a sustainability perspective it is better to develop the knowledge and skills of production than to bring foreign business for product fulfilment.

There is an assumption that bringing a global business to the local will enhance more than just economic activity. However, it is the notion of competition and organizational ethics that we must understand to move through the limiting barriers of sourcing policy. Because of the loss of production due to globalization and the rapid movement of capital, we must rethink what defines community security. Communities also risk homogenization and losing positive attributes of the local business culture.

Reconfiguring the problem presents new perspective. By incorporating the value of social capital, the present opportunities for regaining material and social production by creating collaborative environments between business and community are limitless.

Looking at the discipline of human resources and organizational behaviour, companies are now realizing their number one competitive asset is their labour force. Many companies such as Westjet and Home Depot recognize the importance of motivating and training employees in soft skills and ingenuity. However, their efforts go beyond employee stability policies and approach the ethics and activities of the organization itself. Ikea has gone so far as to design and put into development a sustainable community to demonstrate a future ideal of clean, close living. This ethical stance on business and community is just scratching the surface of potential.

Organizational social capital (OSC) is a resource defined by the strength of ties within the organization. It is built upon common goals, quality of relationships and cohesiveness. The willingness to go the extra mile is a product of social capital. Two attributes define the concept of OSC, associability and trust (Pastoriza, Arino, & Ricart, 2009). Associability refers to the subversion of individualistic behaviour for the common good of the group. Trust is built through a history of personal interactions. This resilience must be fostered through structure and activity, designed and supported by management. OSC is an emergent property of a well functioning organization, in that, no single element of the system, or individual, can produce it. Management sets the tone by supporting and encouraging ethical practices, formal processes, norms and behaviours. Though the individual may come to the organization with well-established norms, the organization will influence the employee's conduct.

Many studies have concluded that the social and moral atmosphere of an organization was a significant factor of influence in positive behaviour (Pastoriza et al., 2009, p. 478). There is no wonder people lack faith in large organizations in today's economic moral climate, and cease to be engaged in creating positive progress. True leaders proactively institute a moral atmosphere that enables greater social capital rather than leave employees to monitor themselves.

Management may take a hard or soft approach to influencing employee behaviour. The hard or structural tools include reward systems, career management streams and job description, and may involve compliance and control techniques. The soft approach is about creating a supportive environment for the employee. Unfortunately, many firms still operate squarely on the hard approach, relying on employee self-interest as the prime motivator. This has the effect of hampering good will within the organization and decreasing the potential of social capital building - and therefore all the intangible benefits such as knowledge transfer, open collaboration and resilience, and of course innovation.

Smart managers realize that "the sources of competitive advantage in their industry will be substantially derived from the capacity of individuals and groups to create value from knowledge by exploiting what they have learned from the past and from exploring new possibilities for the future" (Nahapiet, Gratton, & Rocha, 2005, p. 3). Therefore, it is in the organization's best interest to institute an organizational network based on values. The combination of organizational design and leadership that consistently reinforces a supportive environment in words and actions will yield an equitable and participative team designed around common goals.

93

Anyone familiar with management science will recognize the X-Y theory. The management of individuals who are perceived to be motivated by lower order needs is addressed by Douglas McGregor's X-Y theory, where Theory X tends to view individuals as children who need to be 'micro-managed' and monitored. Those managers with a bias toward Theory Y believes that people are motivated by potential and capacity building for assuming greater responsibility. Theory Y managers believe that the essential task of management is to arrange conditions and methods of operation so people can achieve their own goals. Employee involvement and participation programs, such as Ford Motor Company's, was based on Theory Y assumptions about human behaviour (Sniderman & Nelson, 2007). CSR and good leadership will need a Y manager.

Competition and Collaboration

Programs that engage employees to perform higher-order activities will bring greater satisfaction. Thus, if collaboration is harmony and means the increased ability to access resources such as social capital and knowledge, then conversely competition is disharmony. In this way, competition is can be seen as a psychological flaw, one that limits ability to work together and be creative as a team. No longer is the idea of knowledge management an internal organizational detail but a networked collaborative structure utilizing corporate assets such as information systems and CSR programs. A working functional network means getting the right information to the right people at the right time and is paramount for success in all our institutions.

A closer look at social value creation is needed. To create value is to create relationships, whether it is between a product and a client, a service and a client or an organization and their clients - that sense of community holds value. Community is often associated with the built form of neighbourhood or area and all its holdings, when in fact it has deeper meaning. Community in the social sense is about social structure and building social capital can be worth a lot of revenue and opportunity. Take for instance how people find contracts. They tap into their network and do an environmental scan and query their knowledge sources. They may come up with a 'hit' or two, and their friends or acquaintances provide a tidbit of information that changes the course of events and leads to a job. This is much more powerful and affirmative than chasing newspaper ads.

In *Bowling Alone*, Robert Putnam detailed the de-valuing of social capital in the United States. His research included the study of clubs, organizations and volunteer groups and followed the decrease in memberships and participation in social groups. Many of the assets that are created through networks disappear when the cohesion slips. Building value occurs when relationships are established that assist the brand value and maintain positive competitiveness. Demonstrating the competitive mindset that often accompanies such single-firm/NGO collaborations, CEO Patrick Cescau acknowledged the marketing opportunity associated with ethical responsibilities, stating that the program "provides us a means by which we can differentiate our brands from those of our competitors." (Peloza & Falkenberg, 2009, p. 99)

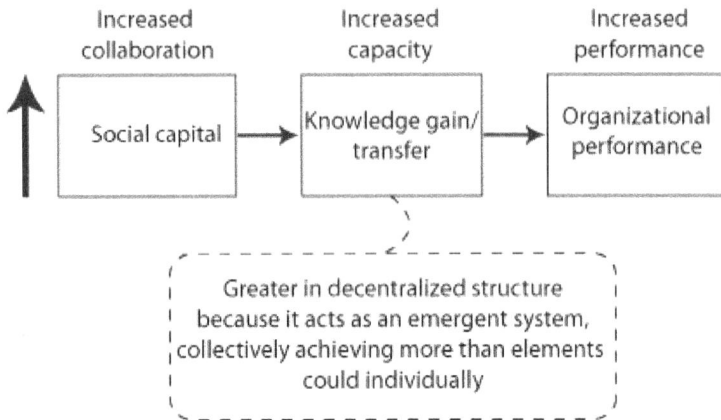

Increased collaboration	Increased capacity	Increased performance
Social capital →	Knowledge gain/ transfer →	Organizational performance

Greater in decentralized structure because it acts as an emergent system, collectively achieving more than elements could individually

In the light of building pro-social behaviour and all the benefits of facilitating personal growth, social capital is an intangible and valuable asset to the organization. When an organization combines monetary reward, feedback and social recognition, performance can improve by up to 45 per cent (Stajkovic & Luthans, 2003).

Promoting the social benefits and marketing with a community perspective builds groups that identify together and this is how word

95

can spread and create links to your business. But the 'word' has to be the positive message that encapsulates your CSR in communications and image. Behaviour modification (BM) can be used to positive affect within an organization. Research suggests that BM positively influenced task performance in both manufacturing and service industries (Sniderman & Nelson, 2007, p. 505). In addition, research revealed that non-financial incentives had impacts on profits and customer service that were as significant as the financial ones in the long term (Ibid).

At the strategic level, creating the links between business operations and social progress requires a systems analysis or a systems approach to depicting the various cycles and operations and the interrelationships between internal and external processes. To underscore the links between CSR and corporate financial performance, Margolis et al found a consistent positive relationship. The conclusions found that there is no compelling evidence to suggest a corporate social program is too costly but that it is costly to be socially irresponsible (Margolis, Elfenbein, & Walsh, 2007). So where do we begin to create social value with a CSR?

Measuring social and environmental performance is necessary for understanding how the organization's activities benefit or harm stakeholders and society. If we focus on outcome and impact, we can pull typical categories found in social responsibility research:

- Disclosure – to fulfil legitimacy or public responsibility or as a response to a wide array of stakeholders
- Environmental impacts – emissions and toxic releases should be accounted and measured for obvious reasons
- Stakeholder specific measures – co-developed community and stakeholder indicators with meaningful outcomes
- Customer and client impacts – measuring perceptions and attitudes toward the organization to develop better understanding of the relationships to financial performance
- Employee satisfaction – examine the perceptions, wellbeing and satisfaction of employees and internal stakeholders and for attracting high-quality job applicants

"Typically the more closely tied a social issue is to a company's business, the greater the opportunity to leverage the firm's resources and benefit society (Porter & Kramer, 2006)". Not surprisingly, many change programs are designed to promote social benefits. New systems of community behaviour are emerging form the interaction of business and community co-developed programs. Increased awareness and use of technology has created and propagated social networks reviling the organization of many large companies. Integrating with these networks can improve corporate response and sensitivity to cultural and social issues.

The overarching question to guide development is 'Where as a community, and as a civilization, do we want to be?' Many societies had answers to those questions for thousands of years, until culture and technology became opposites and it is now a method of adopt and become or be left behind and appear uncompetitive.

Where we want to be becomes a matter of fastest, strongest and most technologically advanced instead of healthy, educated, and harmonious. With the rise of technology and availability, we can sometimes forget that all technology becomes waste and it is merely a tool and not a lifestyle. It is in the learning of technique that we hold personal value and so the learning organization will also be the most progressive. However there are many intangible benefits to group evolution and organizational learning that are rarely expressed as an increase in wealth, one being social capital.

It is not enough to look at the correlation of efforts but also the causality between environmental and social factors and the economic success of the firm. The company will require adjusting new reporting relationships and incentives, examining areas of fragmentation and allowing for a more integrative and affirmative approach.

Establishing a CSR Team

A cohesive team excited by the prospects of positive change should committee the CSR program. Teams are usually formed to deliver specific organizational tasks and goals or to replace management functions. A functional CSR team within an organization can be formed to develop, plan and assess CSR costs and benefits and look for opportunities. Preferably, the team is cross-functional and consists of at least one senior level manager (a sponsor) and people from different departments and strata of the organization. Decisions need to be made when forming the group to increase effectiveness.

Consider the following when forming a team or group:

- Decision-making as a team – will it be a team decision, consensus, or majority vote?
- Sharing of information – face-to-face meetings and electronic communications
- How conflicts will be handled
- The type and frequency of meetings the team will have
- Determining the strengths and weaknesses of the working team and rules of conduct

The team itself should be familiar with good management techniques or be mentored in developing and exploiting core competencies. The core competencies of the firm need to be leveraged and enhanced to competently manage social and environmental investments. Core competencies can enhance the collective learning in the organization, and are especially used to coordinate diverse production skills and integrate multiple streams of technology (Prahalad & Hamel, 1990). Thus, each business unit must develop and maintain it own scorecard to reflect its operational processes and 'what it's good at' with the ability to aggregate upwards into a company profile or report, the CSR program being one aggregation.

A team must also be responsible in terms of accountability. No CSR program is good without the ability to validate and verify results. Third-party verification is available, and independent monitoring and reporting lends more credibility. Over time, competencies can be developed in house and results independently verified by the stakeholders and communities that the program incorporates.

Accountability is necessary to avoid 'green-washing', a term used to describe companies that highlight their public relations efforts yet continue to be involved in unethical practices, something that is still prevalent today. Backwash is also a problem. Initiatives can get started but without the proper momentum and dedication, a team or organization can fall into old habits. A corporation developing its own report card for the purposes of a media campaign is green-washing. Poor performers can design their own metrics with high sounding names, give themselves passing marks and deceive customers and stakeholders (Chatterji & Levine, 2006). This is why transparency is necessary. The public must know and should know about the firm's success in providing leadership in meeting social and environmental challenges.

Corporate Social Strategy Cycle Overview

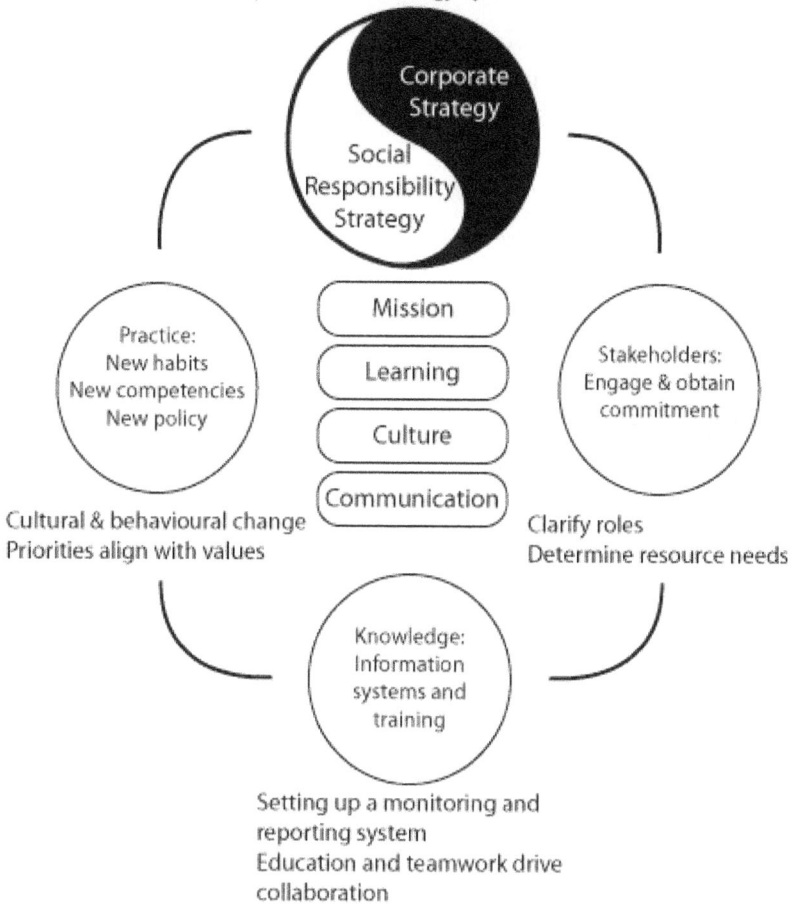

A CSR team may exhibit a new and different set of talents and competencies leading to great value creation. Between years 2001 and 2003, the European Commission, the U.S. Securities and Exchange Commission, and the U.S. Financial Accounting Standards Board commissioned studies that concluded the drivers of wealth for business and the economy are less about physical and financial assets than about intangibles such as intellectual property and employee talent. Having a strong social responsibility program attracts and retains talented people who recognize the business cares and has a voice in the way it conducts its daily business. Among other notable benefits:

- CSR imbues professionalism and good conduct

- It reduces costs
- It creates efficiencies
- It improves employee satisfaction
- It improves the health of stakeholders and the environment
- It sparks innovation
- It gives credibility and social licence to operate
- It helps manage the business through greater introspection

As you can see, a true CSR goes beyond doing a 'bit' for the environment. It is a tool and strategy that can reinvent a business, consistently and progressively for the benefit of business and client. Employing a CSR and integrating it into the core competencies of an organization can bring long-term security, reduced risk and greater market acceptance.

A purpose is always more compelling than a goal.

Talented employees are those that are able to express their strengths and unique abilities to create change and progress in their respective roles. This can be in the form of divergent thinking, creative direction, analytical skills, people skills, and leadership. But there is not an infinite pool available for sourcing talent, it must be recognized and nurtured and appreciated. After studying high-performance companies, management scholars Charles O'Reilly and Jeffrey Pfeffer conclude that success is achieved because those companies are better than their competitors at getting extraordinary results from the people working for them (Schermerhorn, 2008).

Competition is fierce for those with proven abilities or skills that are much sought after in every discipline. CSR is compelling to those who wish to use their abilities to feel like they are doing more than producing widgets for the sake of producing widgets; people want to contribute. CSR says 'we care about you, the employees, your health and your communities'. Jim Copeland, Jr., former CEO of Deloitte Touche Tohmatsu, puts it this way: "The best professionals in the world want to work in organizations in which they can thrive, and they want to work for companies that exhibit good corporate citizenship (Bhattacharya, Sen, & Korschun, 2008).

Enabling CSR becomes an internal HR and marketing tool and even a strategic imperative to develop a strong resilient organization, retain employees and increase productivity. This is because CSR is an approach that necessarily develops the positive behaviour in people, thereby developing their strengths rather than the traditional HR approach of managing weaknesses. The key is for management to understand and market CSR to the different employee segments. Corporate social marketing programs, corporate philanthropy and support for social initiatives can all be perceived quite differently and so the barriers and opportunities must be understood.

The team must form a campaign or charter for the program. Bhattacharya, Sen and Korshun found four areas that can act as barriers to an effective CSR campaign:

1. Employees are kept at 'arm's length' when communicating the details of the CSR program;
2. A CSR program may not consider the diverse sets of needs for employees;
3. Companies do not understand the value of the psychological benefits arising from a good CSR, such as pro-company behaviours, increased productivity, and longer tenures;
4. Employing a top-down hierarchal mandatory approach rather than a participatory approach

Communicating and promoting the CSR is critical to overcoming the varying degrees that employees may be aware of a company's social initiatives. Even when employees become aware of the CSR program they may find it difficult to access additional information for follow up. These are missed opportunities to engage with employees, build the intangible assets and creating an active involvement culture. Meeting employees' needs goes beyond benefits packages, and vary in type and degree. The success of job role is reliant on higher-order psychological needs as well. Employees seek opportunities for personal growth in a job role and may find it in becoming an active part of a CSR program, whether its volunteering, community outreach or learning more about the business practices. Skills developed through engagement practices translate in greater effectiveness on the job.

Work-life balance is crucial to happiness and wellbeing. Integrating work and community initiatives creates the intrinsic bond, improves transition and shows that the company respects personal values as much as employees. Dissolving the separation between work life and community lowers stress and builds social capital. CSR can create more opportunities for employees to connect with each other on meaningful levels. Building bonds internally and with remote employees is important to wellbeing. This translates into greater acceptance and more productive team work.

CSR can also combat the negative impressions that external stakeholders may have about a company's practices or poor performance record. The process of developing and being a part of something good within the company brings pride and esteem to the job, develops commitment and morale among employees and their roles. CSR is an excellent marketing and promotional word of mouth and online opportunity. Few companies take the time and develop the systems and measures necessary to gain insight into employee process and outcomes that stem from their CSR initiatives. Poor evaluation of feedback degrades performance and creates missed opportunities for continual enhancement.

Good Relationships is Good Business

Any strategic approach to CSR will warrant greater participation by employees to induce the positive benefits previously mentioned. Embracing employees into the CSR program requires clear and concise communications backed by credibility about the types of activities, the resources allocated and the challenges and successes anticipated by the program.

"Employees also noted that their employer's commitment to socially responsible behaviour inspires them to work harder, be more productive and focus more on quality."
— Female, Regional Office of Consumer-Goods Company (Bhattacharya et al., 2008, p. 41)

103

Building Strategic Partners

Exchanging resources and expertise is invaluable. Collaborative relationships bring competitive advantage and increase social capital. For achieving combined economic and societal goals, many corporations large and small seek the expertise and drive of NGOs to further their causes. Such partnerships include Coca-Cola and WWF, McDonalds and the Environmental Defence Fund, Starbucks and Oxfam, Nike and the Fair Labour association. The list goes on and includes one-on-one relationships as well as multi-firm and multi-NGO collaborations. The need to partner reveals the cross-pollination of skills and knowledge that an NGO and a business need to share, since NGOs are already organized to address social issues.

Due to the complexity of social problems, an increased interaction among previously disconnected sectors will close knowledge gaps. Only when we combine government, non-government and the private sector will we be recognizing our problems in a meaningful way. A true wide scale, wide reaching program may be considered social enterprise; applying business and market mechanisms to make social progress. By creating a cross-sector social enterprise, a new organization or complex adaptive system is formed, one that has new potential for innovation. The potential can be unleashed if there if intellect, desire and foresight to induce structural change to enhance the new interactions that will take place. Learning enhancement is characteristic of good relationships, allowing all partners to benefit from feedback. In a learning world there is no failure, only feedback.

In forming a relationship, businesses will focus on a narrow objective and assign specific resources. Innovation cannot take place in a restricted environment, so the organization will have to reflect its desire for innovation throughout its organization. Innovation does require trying new things and experimenting with methods and behaviours. When CSR partnerships are formed, there is an explicit contract in order to 'make better' a social problem that needs addressing. The missed opportunities often exist in the impacts that a collaboration effort can have to change each partner or the entire industry (Seitanidi, 2008). This is due to the dynamics of the relationship formed by the act of donation or sponsorship, creating a one-way report and address relationship. A true relationship, one where real innovation will flourish, must be a mutually assumed reporting responsibility, one that will reveal the benefits and reverberate throughout an industry.

It is hard to grasp that failure is institutionalized within business organizations, that every business that strives to make a profit is also cutting its own throat by not being part of the grand solution to issues that require concerted effort. The responsibility of business to 'fit in' with the needs of society and environment has evaporated, mostly due to lack of ability to adapt and lack of foresight.

Organizations can be built to succeed, not just in short-term profits but in long-term sustainability, by naturally forming around a CSR core mandate. Reorganizing for a CSR culture will plant the seeds for sustainable growth. Self-organizing systems do not occur spontaneously as some might like to conjecture, but require the right conditions to evolve. A structure forms and functions still manifest, and all is not chaos when a system is allowed to function freely. There is a natural settlement to circumstances that occurs when elements are left to operate as intended. The special interests that feel a need to control an organization can also hinder it by suppressing emergent qualities. Sometimes the best thing for a leader to do is get out of the way.

Again, we come back to emergent properties and how special functions can only come to fruition as a sum of the whole and not its parts. What leaders can do is tweak the system to allow new possibilities rather than leave it to chance or some reactive process. Partnerships also occur on the micro-level within the internals of the organization. Employees and suppliers are valuable and willing assistants to contribute to a shared values initiative. By engaging employees and suppliers as partners you reach further into their being than simple contractual obligation. Some of the most valuable contributions may be missed just because they are not offered. The best plans include purpose, process and passion.

Managing for Quality

The economy is moving from a mass quantity, production and consume model to a quality, maintenance and service model. To give an example, many people have laundry machines at home and spend much time and energy doing their families wash. A move towards a quality model would mean finding a laundry service that uses top quality machines and service models. Thus, the cost savings to the family translates into a service. This means less things in the house, more space, less maintenance, more time, and businesses benefit from more customers, greater employment and investment. All of this translates into less landfill, less pollution and a more responsible economy. Quality is doing more with less while enhancing the well being for the organization.

Doing more with less does not mean squeezing existing resources to maximize output. Using less reduces waste and all of the waste we produce embodies lost labour, energy, materials, chemicals, transport, wear and tear and land. By eliminating waste we are automatically becoming more efficient but that is only half of the sustainable operations. Doing more means taking action, and putting the effort in to being a top performer in environmental management. It means education and adoption, experimentation and failure and team success.

All businesses should be familiar with *Industrial Ecology*. Industrial Ecology is a term that represents that closing of business input and output loops. For example, the cradle-to-grave analogy is used to describe a business perspective on its product life cycle, while a cradle-to-cradle perspective looks at the materials cycle to the point where it is reconstituted for material input once again, saving primary resource extraction, energy, waste and pollution. Many business leaders are aware of former CEO of Interface Flooring, Ray Anderson's efforts to minimize waste and pollution that came as a result from reading Paul Hawking's book, 'The Ecology of Commerce'. This was a revelation for Anderson as he looked at his business in a new light, seeing the connections between what the firm was doing and the destruction of the planet.

I highlight the automobile as the most successful product ever developed. We experience all the benefits of mobility and pay a great deal to be able to get around in gas, insurance, maintenance, but rarely acknowledge the other impacts. Paul Hawken, Amory Lovins and L. Hunter Lovins have detailed some points about the automobile and its impacts in their recent book, Natural Capitalism (2009). Among these consequences are:

- America has paved and area of arable land equal to the states of Ohio, Indiana, and Pennsylvania, requiring $200 million of maintenance per day
- Created a social justice issue in designing communities that restrict the mobility of children and elders
- Maimed or injured 250 million people; more than all the Americans who have died in all the wars of the countries history
- Burning 8 million barrels of oil every day
- Create increasing dependence and hostility around the world for resources
- Killing a million animals per week, from deer to elk, birds, frogs and domestic pets

Energy-wise, these numbers will astound you as to the waste this product produces:

- Of all the fuel the car consumes, at least 80 per cent is lost as heat and exhaust so that at most 20 per cent is actually used to turn the wheels
- 95 per cent of the force of combustion moves the car, while only 5 per cent actually moves the driver (Hawken, Lovins, & Lovins, 1999)

These points underscore the inefficiency of the car even though we have a love affair with this most successful product. Choice in mobility is also responsible for our sense of freedom. But acknowledging our problem, like an alcoholic or drug addict is the first step to real freedom. Today, progress is being defined in the automobile industry by leaders such as Toyota. Years ago, they had seen the future and placed a large investment into the electric-hybrid, which in time has given them the competitive advantage to become the number one car company in the world. Toyota is not just a car company but is in the business of transportation systems, embracing the integrated approach to society and its needs by also fulfilling orders in light rail systems and efficient motor supply. No doubt, problems will still arise, but the general direction has been set and the vision created. Although industries such as oil and gas may not desire improvements that castrate their own sales, technological disruption has always created opportunities; consequently suppression of technology has led to oppression or monopolistic tendencies.

When materials cannot be food for another system, products need to be designed to be broken down into their component parts and re-used for other purposes. This moves away from planned obsolescence. Disposal into anything not fully digestible for use in any other process is harmful waste. The more systems that can digest the by-product of our economy, the more valuable the leftovers are to the point where it can generate more revenue than costs and thus a whole new clean economy. Designing for digestion, whether its human re-use or natural process is quality management.

Corporate responsibility includes creating and taking advantage of efficiencies – some quite obvious - that will result in reduced social and environmental impacts. Reducing waste is a key factor and underscores what it means to employ quality management. Many firms look towards energy and resource savings in what is termed 'eco-efficiency'. Eco-efficiency on its own will not propel a firm into the new market sphere or make it stand out as a leader, but it is absolutely necessary in order to make progress in unnecessary resource consumption. Eco-efficiency is really an exercise in accounting for waste but *industrial ecology is a philosophy that drives a vision for the organization.*

Eco-efficiency can be realized by the application of technology and a change in behaviour. Technologies are applied to operations and processes to capture heat, water or other resources that would have gone to the end of the pipe or released into the environment. This application has costs, but realizes paybacks, especially as resources and commodities increase in price and become scarce. Look to green buildings and the application of leading edge design principles. Even if you are working in an existing infrastructure, much can be done to reduce impacts to health and environment. The health and safety committee would do well to understand energy use and green building methods, volatile chemical compounds, diet and nutrition needs and track well being indicators for staff.

Organizational behavioural change is necessary to embrace the application of new technology and create a culture of conservation, creating more savings and bringing a communal purpose to new development and innovation. Any CSR program should account for the company's and associated partners' operational waste and resource consumption patterns. Typically, an examination of supply chain and building site performance will set the indicators for the eco-efficiency portion of the program. Unless a company articulates a waste reduction program, it will be exposed to more risk as the 'polluter pays more' policies become an increasingly popular way of ensuring clean up of our environment.

Much of the incentive for improving operations and waste management lies in savings. Tax incentives can be created for those who invest in environmental quality improvements. In Hong Kong, businesses who invest capital expenditure into environmental protection technologies can be 100 per cent deducted under the new green tax incentive, whether its improvements on buildings or machinery for the purposes of air or water quality or noise reduction (Chan, 2009). Environmental improvements include:

- Solar panels or solar water heating
- Wind turbine installations
- Landfill gas installations
- Anaerobic digestion installations
- Thermal waste treatment installations
- Wave power installations
- Hydroelectric installations
- Bio-fuel installations
- Bio-mass combined heat and power (CHP) installations

109

- Geothermal installations
- (Some) Green building improvements

Environmental and social improvements can reduce risk to the organization. We use the term risk to sum up the chances of an event negatively impacting a system. For businesses, risk is in the form of competition, rising costs and now resource scarcity, climate change, and employee health as a result of external factors such as food security, air quality, stress from commuting, etc. There is also risk that appears in the form of codes and legislation.

As social and environmental quality changes, institutions and businesses are expected to react themselves, and to ensure there is compliance. When market forces fail, regulation may be used. Research shows businesses that are forward thinking and minimize risk early on, benefit far greater than those who react to change (Henriques & Sadorsky, 1999). Lowering risk through a CSR program could keep a company from experiencing boycott attacks, loss of talented employees, NGO criticism, and government impositions (Mainelli, 2004). Lowering risk also includes increasing value by brand enhancement, retaining talent, and sharing in positive relations with NGOs and government.

Thinking on eco-efficiency can be cognatively dissonant. On one hand, efficiency means saving resources, on the other it is increasing our rates of production far past the earth's ability to cope with the demand. Efficiency in this way is a dual-edged sword. Making progress in closed-loop systems between production and waste is the only real-world efficiency that would work in the long-term.

Employing Change Management

"People do not resist change, they resist being changed." - Richard Beckhard

The term 'Change Management' is redundant because, in fact, everything changes. It is how we mitigate and progress that dictates the benefits of change and the state of mind of those involved.

Change management needs to be a core competency of the organization rather than an incremental project based on a reaction to external influences. There is no more time for the go-slow approach. Basic business management strategy stresses the importance of understanding rate of change and complexity in the environment. However, businesses need the skills to successfully mitigate change and a path for becoming a learning organization.

Change management is arguably an action research task of performing constant environmental scanning, creating information from data gathering, and creating knowledge that is then acted upon in such a way as to be able to create positive transformation. This continual pro-activity ensures accurate intelligence and creates a better atmosphere for innovation. Depending on the organizational competencies in change strategy, you may either be changed by external forces or lead the change.

There are two types of change for an organization: process and product. Change to internal processes is driven by top management, supported by the drive of a bottom-up participatory approach. Participation and empowerment for employees is crucial in allowing those who know best to do their job best. A worker becomes a knowledge worker by being encouraged to seek alternatives that could save money or time and in doing so, becomes a greater asset to the organization.

Change in organizational members can be initiated through coaching and mentoring. The manager may play the role of coach or may bring in a consultant versed in methods of organizational change and performance enhancement. Coaching can also be brought in to assist management with the development of leadership skills through visioning, counselling and new ideas to stimulate progress toward objectives. Using such techniques as Appreciative Inquiry (AI) can yield great results in setting a positive and motivational vision.

The psychology of change is important in determining effectiveness of a change program. The popular Lewin's model depicts in simplicity, the opposing forces of status quo and necessary change.

Recognizing change is a process, preparation is necessary and a plan that recognizes why the change is taking place. The change may challenge long held beliefs and values and so communication must explain why the current methods cannot continue.

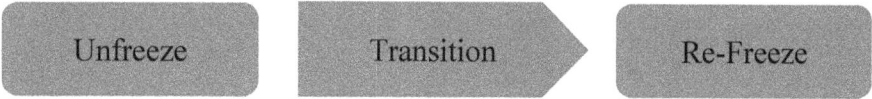

Unfreeze → Transition → Re-Freeze

The fear of change may creat insecurity, make it feel as if a crisis is occurring, but this is a controlled and planned event and change is a natural part of process and growth. Resistance to change exists in every formal and informal structure. Fear is the biggest barrier for people when it comes time to take a leap of faith or take a chance, even a calculated risk can seem like doomsday. Much of the fear is psychosomatic, however, it still needs to be understood and addressed, because fear can stagnate and paralyze an organization.

Fear, in the organizational context is the opposite of learning – it is a paralyzer. For progress to be made, something new must replace something old. Fear wants to hold onto anything it thinks is secure, even if it is detrimental in the long run. This can be because the individual may feel they will lose power or influence during or after the change, or perhaps the changes will deem them incompetent as they have long mastered the old ways but are unfamiliar with the new.

In transition, support is built for the new vision. New and stronger connections can be made to the new mandate. It is imperative people are part of the change process. Use of people skills, communications and mentorship will allow for freedom of expression, concerns or ideas. Affirm the small successes and relieve confusion by addressing it head on, be sure, and work together.

Change management extends beyond the internal re-jigging of the organization. Change also involves the people and communities with which the program seeks to develop. A successful CSR change campaign will aim to establish a *community enterprise*, the promotion of 'trade for social purpose', which creates conditions for earned income rather than philanthropic hand-outs or government subsidy (Nwankwo et al., 2007). "Community enterprises are non-profit organizations [where] surpluses are re-invested in the business or communities they serve. They therefore combine social and commercial objectives, …and are often described as a hybrid form of organization" (p. 97).

This form of co-operative has structured governance, an elected board of trustees and participatory processes that engages local citizenry for determining the strategic direction. This brings a sense of empowerment and purpose. With this structure in place, new cost and project sharing options become available. The business can lend assistance in skills, resources and project management, while local knowledge and initiative is performed by the enterprise.

Advantages to forming a community enterprise include being recognized as a valid form of organization that can apply for grants, funds and programs eligible for fund matching from firms. The enterprise acts as a business, accepting fiscal and social responsibility yet retaining the ability to legitimately respond to the desires and needs of the community. Developing and working with community enterprises as a form of positive social change goes beyond the typical CSR model, allowing communities to direct and manage resources where usually a corporations well-meaning actions would make the decisions.

Recognize the constraints to change and depict the work culture to better grasp where paralysis or resistance exists. The culture within an organization may support 'sameness' rather than diversity, in thinking and behaving. This is usually due to the long-term dis-involvement of the business with outside entities. It is like meeting someone who has not had the opportunity to travel and experience other cultures. The mind will remain closed to new experiences if it does not have trust in its own coping skills.

Change can feel like it is giving up values or compromising individual beliefs that are linked to one's personal identity. It may be that some individuals may feel the new mandate is not for them. For this same reason, this is why new radicals are socially penalized for

113

thinking outside the box. They introduce a creative disruption that is so far removed from the routines of the group or organizational thought process. If the organization is closed to new thinking or fearful of change, the entrepreneurial drive that characterizes free thinking and individuality is wasted. This is why successful diversity planning introduces conditions for innovation. Allowing for exploration brings new enterprise. The acceptance of other cultures, thoughts, ideas, and perspectives stimulates dialogue and interaction. Multi-culturalism 'think-alism' works but only if people work together.

Bringing people together for the purposes of change requires a charismatic and thoughtful leader to communicate a compelling positive vision. People must be motivated to engage with the learning and contribute to the outcomes. Provide support and training as part of a new system that encourages criticism and ideas so that the group can move forward adaptively and begin thinking in new and positive ways. Do not underestimate the power of organizational learning as it can fundamentally change norms and beliefs and thus the behaviours of each individual within the program. Once new understandings are reinforced and internalized, free enterprise can occur on the new levels of insight, creating a positive contribution to organizational progress. Coaching also becomes more effective because delegating responsibility has greater capacity and spectrum in which to operate, alleviating leaders of the 'micro-management' syndrome that can create a distaste for management interference.

To facilitate a change program, the cultural assumptions and perspectives have to be known. Edgar Schein has designed a problem solving exercise that should involve a group of people (10-15) involved with the issue.

- The facilitator should be an outside person that is assisting the change agent inside the organization.
- The environment should be a comfortable face-to-face meeting.
- Properly define the problem with the premise of improving some facet of the organization's strategy or performance.

- Examine and discuss the cultural environment and how it is expressed in the built form, the organization's ethics and values and long-standing assumptions within the work culture.
- List all the symbols and cultural artefacts the group points out that characterize the organization (i.e. dress code, level of formality, meetings, live work balance, communication, reward systems, social events, conflict resolution methods, etc.)
- Identify the organization's explicit values whether expressed in vision, mission statements, current initiatives.
- Compare the explicit values with the organizational artefacts and see if they align. If not, the cultural assumption and internal value system is driving the system. For example, open communication may be promoted openly but critics and whistle-blowers are punished. Inconsistencies between behaviour and organization vision and communications need to be highlighted.
- Assess how the basic assumptions will help or hinder the posed business or organizational problem. Push for the positive but plan for barriers.
- Decide on next steps whether it's the initial strategy discussion or a continued information gathering agenda. There may be other groups that have to be cross-checked that could help you validate your initial findings. Develop any plans using the cultural strengths and competencies and where they will be used in a change program. Identify how to overcome any perceived barriers.
- Develop a proposal for change.

Embedding a CSR program into an organization's culture requires a sympathetic and holistic change program to encapsulate the CSR objectives. Going beyond the traditional CSR report and initiatives that characterize sporadic attempts at displaying values but not living them, will motivate staff and create a positive culture.

Facilitating Change

•Use group sessions to discover the cultural values and assumption
•Properly define the problem or challenges to the organization through group work
•Align cultural strengths to the new strategy and potential impacts of cultural barriers

This section will highlight the most important points in considering and framing your CSR initiative for your organization and expand in detail the background and steps to developing the program.

Implementing the CSR Program

"Successful corporations need a healthy society" – Porter & Kramer

The CSR design and implementation process remains mostly unexplored (Maon, Lindgreen, & Swaen, 2009). Typically, practitioners will adhere to a business plan model, outlining the objectives, resources, and timelines, but guidance on a cultural remodelling goes beyond project management. It starts with a clear understanding of the needs and direction of stakeholders, a firm strategy and a change management plan all of which is built on the premise of adaptive management. We have previously discussed group exercises around determining organizational cultural assets and how they can be aligned to a strategy for problem solving. Now it is time to get on with the broader approach.

In formulating the strategy, consideration for stakeholder input, employee engagement, health and wellbeing improvements, and learning opportunities for continuous improvement in process and profit should be highlighted. Main activities include preparation, transformation, implementation, and review.

An initial snapshot of organizational standing, with respect to CSR, is required to gauge progress. Information needs to be gathered on:

1) social and environmental performance, including impacts
2) corporate governance issues
3) commitment to sustainability
4) current practice with respect to stakeholder dialogue

Once a 'temperature' is taken, the building of trust and dialogue can begin to form a collaborative basis for building the CSR program. A good CSR program is one that promotes health and safety in the broader context and attracts and retains talent because of its mandate. It can become a competitive advantage by having a strategic position that will influence innovation.

Broad steps:

- Select objectives and goals
- Identify priority areas in the business for operational and social progress
- Engage employees to understand community and global concerns
- Identify core competencies
- Identify stakeholder groups
- Engage and prioritize social issues
- Re-select objectives, goals and integrate performance measures

The business will have to organize a range of activities into discrete projects, preferably a range of small investment and experiments. The projects should have some metrics to evaluate progress and investment over the long-term. These types of projects are not conventional short-term discounted cash-flow yields nor long-term R&D investments but rather what Hart and Milstein call 'Real-options thinking which introduces the logic of the private equity market with an payback outlook of 5-7 years (Hart, Milstein, & Caggiano, 2003). Developing a separate fund and entity will manage these projects easier lest it fall victim to the short-term thinking of typical business operations.

The framework for assessing the performance of CSR needs to be understood before the CSR is launched. In more detailed fashion, Phillip Kotler, distinguished professor of International Marketing, and Nancy Lee (Kotler & Lee, 2005) list several points that should be considered to employ best practices in developing a CSR. Below is a partial list and some additional points added for emphasis:

- Focus only on key issues and communities from which your organization can most benefit
- Find causes that share the same mission and values or mesh well with your products and services
- Choose causes that have potential to enhance business productivity, relations, or marketing
- Develop a case that is attractive to all stakeholders
- Find partners that are strong and committed to meeting the same objectives
- Form a cross-functional team to develop plans
- Form a stakeholder group that includes community
- Establish and communicate clear and measurable objectives
- Get senior management buy-in
- Create a reporting structure and algorithm with appropriate indicators
- Become expert in the issues your organization is addressing – know the issues enough to lecture on them
- Keep people engaged – it is easy to fall of the table when energy or resources are low

By engaging different stakeholder groups a firm can leverage all the resources and wealth of knowledge that comes with an extended network. Community members are sometimes particularly keen to develop a CSR agenda that could positively impact the community. Students and interns scramble for the opportunities that could be yielded from developing new programs, and universities want to work with business to experiment and apply its new theories and practices.

The opportunity to form a community enterprise must be explored during implementation.

The learning opportunities for the firm can be reciprocated. The initial coming together and brainstorming produces an energy that should overcome inertia to create and inspire others to get involved, replicating the success.

Visualizing goals and objectives

Where there is no vision, the people perish –Solomon Proverbs 29:18

A compelling vision is important on many levels, individual and group, as well as societal. As the above proverb suggests, a lack of vision creates indeterminate goals and strategies, which lead to nowhere. CSR helps create, and is created through, vision by working with motivations and values that will lead progress in business and personal development. Visioning exercises inclusive of employees, clients, investors or other key stakeholders will ensure that their vested interests remain applicable.

Clear strategies are ones that are easily understood and accepted by all participants and members of an organization. Stakeholder involvement in developing strategy develops buy-in and social licence to execute. The strategic vision is one that can grow organically and become a symbiotic partnership with stakeholder communities. Strategies that are developed in isolation carry greater risk and may develop adversity to project objectives.

Many psychometric tools and assessment methods have been developed for stakeholder engagement. Appreciative Inquiry (AI) is one such example that would meet the needs of management for the purposes of creating a positive vision for change management. How many times have consultants been hired, policies been made and materials created that have had little or no impacts? Clearly this represents a waste of time and money. AI offers a much more sincere and positive approach without excluding any tools that could be used to better understand employee motivations.

Coaching or facilitating an AI session needs the hearts and minds of individuals and members of the organization to be involved with a new inspirational vision. They will see themselves, their roles, and the organization as a dynamic, life-giving purposeful organization that is a world-class leader and among the most desirable places to work. The facilitator needs to introduce the Appreciative Inquiry process, setting the purpose and project out with clear communications. Choose someone in house that has experience and is open to working with others critique and apathy. Raising motivation levels and inspiring others is needed to bring out the creative aspects of the type of thinking and visioning that will lead the process.

In an appreciative inquiry process, there is no project that is done, but rather an inclusive inquiry of the employees who are the process. Engagement uncovers the barriers and desires of the members of the organization in order to raise performance and satisfaction. AI is employed to create an exciting and dynamic organization using positive psychology. Benefits include:

- Co-creating a vision and strategy for the future
- Accelerate organizational learning
- Improve communications and dialog
- Develop a culture of innovation and sustainability
- Build great relationships with trust and rapport

As part of the discovery process, several interviews will take place with individuals to allow for the freedom of expression for sincere and honest feedback. Feelings of hope, frustration and possibly anger and fear may surface during this time. Allow all feedback, critique and negativity about the workplace to come out. For positive change to occur, one must be open and honest about how one feels if progress is to be made. To be effective, the process must remain positive and visionary, engaging the best and most creative elements of each person in the interview.

Appreciative inquiry also finds its role in building organizational capacity, relationship building, knowledge management and socially responsible enterprises. It remains a practice that seeks to change behaviours and attitudes and thus practice through dialog and relationships, creating interaction to bring out the best in people. It allows for putting the human back into 'human resources'. Developing a combined vision of the future that is hopeful, dynamic and good for everyone underpins the heuristic component. We learn as we go with the future in mind and are motivated and influenced by the anticipation of success in creating a better, healthier more prosperous world.

Human systems move toward the direction of exploration, curiosity and motivation. This brings meaning and purpose to change. Discovering purpose in one's life and as a group or collective is an exhilarating experience. The drive to succeed comes from a good place. Aim for uncovering purpose during the inquiry process. Key questions are to be used with the individuals, team members and their selected partners. It allows them to open up and provide interesting ideas and visions. Keep the questions short when engaging and keep the energy moving.

Leading the Workshop

A workshop session will be needed to facilitate the vision process. Appreciative inquiry workshops can last from one hour to two days. Prepare and agenda for anywhere from a one- to two hour inquiry. You may want to subtract or add your own learning or coaching modules that have been successfully been used in the past.

Select your stakeholders

Involve senior managers, committee members, staff, strategic partners and community enterprise members. The greater the bandwidth in stakeholders the wider perspectives and greater contribution can be expected. One of the goals of inquiry is to get diverse opinions and create dialogue.

The first step of the AI process will be identifying the 'life-affirming' factors for the focus of the inquiry. Topic selection will guide the entire process.

Examining the Organizational Culture

In interviews, make note of language terms and visual cues and in what context, informal (hallways, lunch room, local pub) or formal environment such as a meeting. You may find that language used to describe work changes is dependent on the environmental setting.

Examine the history and the strength of legacy within the organization. Are people valued for their work and experience? Are the success stories shared among all members? Find the best stories by looking for openness, positive future outlook, positive qualities mentioned in selves and others.

Selecting Topics

Choose the themes for change. Select 3-5 topics for the inquiry process. Human systems move in the direction of inquiry. This will impact the vision, language and culture, so it is important everyone participates and that a diversity of interest is expressed. Build a steering committee or a senior-executive team. Engage the whole system if possible. Topics must be:

- No more than five selected
- Stated in positive language
- Aligned with vision and intention of the organization
- Create a genuine curiosity
- Engages those with a stake in the future of the organization
- No more than two days

The following is an adaptation of 4-D process designed by David Cooperider, Diana Whitney, and Jacqueline Stavros. This bright and fabulous way of steeping through the process engages and structures the most important components of the inquiry. They are aptly named:

The Discovery Phase - Look for highlights in peak performance and organizational excellence. This will identify the keys to unlocking future success by pinpointing the tools, leadership skills, rapport conditions, processes and communications used in past great experiences.

The Dream Phase - Inquires about whose future it is and to create mutual life-giving images of the future. Reach for a balanced approach that strikes a work-life balance, economic, social and environmental progress. This is about raising potential.

The Design Phase - The social architecture is crafted in this phase. The elements must be decided on and include leadership, strategy, organizational culture, human resources management, client relations, and community involvement. This is about connecting and strengthening the web of relationships to enhance the quality of organizational life.

The Destiny Phase - This phase structures the planning and commitment from each stakeholder for their contribution to realizing the articulations captured from the design phase. At this time, sustaining the momentum for change may require altering surveys, training programs, performance measurement metrics and diversity initiatives. New processes or changes in existing systems may be necessary to meet the design phase propositions.

Potential benefits to stakeholder engagement in the visioning process include enhancing the planning process by gaining insight into potential barriers and other unknown variables, thereby accelerating the needed change. Building resilience by addressing both long term and short term planning initiatives with stakeholders may be the difference of an organization surviving an economic or societal shift. Developing a legacy of loyalty by proactively soliciting stakeholders ideas and vision for organizational direction will retain employees and social resources that can be called upon when needed. Leaders will need to re-evaluate visions to align and with emerging societal and environmental issues. It is a good idea to start creating a checklist of everything mentioned so you can customize your agenda and plan.

Sort out the long-term vision factors to guide the short-term steps so that the compass reads in the proper direction. Explicit language and common goals will set the foundation for the change management.

Adaptability and leadership will light the path while information, communication and engagement provides the inertia. Here are examples of some strategic steps and questions to ask within your team or organization:

Identify organizational mission and objectives
What business are we in?
Where do we want to go?

Assess current performance in comparison with the missions and objectives
How well are we doing?

Create the strategic plans to accomplish the purpose and objectives
How can we get where we want and NEED to be?

Implement the strategic plans:
Has everything been done that needs to be done?
Are there new options that could work within the existing framework?

Evaluate results and change plans or processes to fine-tune for improvement:
Are things working out as planned?
Where can improvements be made?

A good mission statement identifies the domain in which the organization intends to operate and includes the customers, products, services, communities and location in which it wants to serve and operate. The statement must be realizable and relevant to stakeholders, which include employees, shareholders, customers, suppliers, communities or anyone (and anything) that is directly affected by an organization and its accomplishments. The mission becomes real and relevant to society when it encapsulates the true values of the members. What the organization is trying to accomplish must align with stakeholders, resource availability, culture and reality.

In setting priorities and bringing vision, consider these aspects and influences:

Inspiration – make your statement bold enough to inspire others
Achievements – highlight success and push for something new
Management – get a good picture of the management culture
Staff – what personal ideals resonate with the organizations core values
Suppliers – what can be achieved by working more closely with suppliers
Government – engage local and regional policy
Costs – what are the initial costs of such a vision
Benefits – explicitly define and communicate the benefits
Challenges – List potential barriers to adoption and success
Future – always look to what's next to keep the inertia going

Almost every company with aspirations of profitability and growing market share has a mission or a vision statement. They have a mission because they believe they will be around in the long run. Does it help anything or anyone if the vision is short sighted? Will it just be a plaque on the wall or a commitment to good work? Considering the business in relation with society and environment, it is more necessary for a business to have an '*Intention Statement*'. More concrete than vision and more clear than a mission statement, an intention statement directs people with an ethic not just an objective. Intention is imbued with creativity and intelligence, an appealing mix that motivates, and inspires innovation. The rest is just following through.

Go beyond setting the mission and deliver an honest intention – it has more force and meaning to your organization and community.

Defining the Stakeholders

No business can exist in a bubble. In fact, globalization and technology have thrust business into a complex media and information web with institutions and community. Those that hide business activities are usually held to the strongest criticism. Those that successfully define their primary stakeholders and what their interests are in the business activities are well positioned to develop new strategies. So what do we look for in a stakeholder?

For stakeholder engagement to be relevant and a worthwhile investment, stakeholders need to be identified and sussed out. There is a spectrum of stakeholder types that will enhance business and community engagement without over-taxing management with queries or unnecessary attention. The good stakeholder recognizes a good business and invests time and energy just as the business would to further mutual goals for social and environmental stewardship.

Freeman's definition of stakeholder is – 'any group or individual who can affect or is affected by the achievement of the organization's objectives' (Strategic Management: A Stakeholder Approach, 1984). A stakeholder may also be defined as those groups "on which the organization is dependent on for its continued survival" (Stanford Research Institute, 1963). What precisely is at 'stake' and who has a 'stake' is ultimately decided by the agreement of the interest group and the business owners. This also leaves a wide spectrum of types of stakeholder: owners and non-owners, owners of tangible or intangible assets, voluntary or involuntary relationships with the business, suppliers, buyers, lawyers and agents. The business will have to determine the most relevant and best stakeholders for engaging.

Mitchell, Agle and Wood propose classifying stakeholders by three attributes:

1) the stakeholder's power to influence the firm
2) the legitimacy of the stakeholder's relationship with the firm, and;
3) the urgency of the stakeholder's claim on the firm (Mitchell, Agle, & Wood, 1997).

Using this typology, we can understand why managers when set out to achieve certain objectives pay certain kinds of attention to some stakeholders rather than others. The interests and claims of non-shareholding groups are increasingly becoming the responsibility of senior management. Thus, understanding the roles and relationships is crucial to successful mediation. A stakeholder does bear some form of risk as a result of some form of capital in the firm, be it human or financial, or as a result of the firm's activities.

Maintaining and engaging stakeholders with timely information, keeps the mandate relevant. Stakeholders in the information age have taken the participatory approach for social agendas to new areas of engagement such as social media. Online information gathering and interaction can be in one of three states for a stakeholder: 1) information posting and digestion; 2) information gathering in the form of a survey or profiling and search criteria, and; 3) instant messaging and feedback. Information posting would be the form of an electronic document or a web page, typically produced dynamically from a content-managed system. The user or stakeholder is able to locate and download the information that allows them to be informed and participate in some form. Collection of personal details, demographics, location or address and contact information (email is particularly important) is necessary to provide the most relevant information.

Information gathering, as with such services as feedback forms or online polls allow collection of research data through quantitative and qualitative reactions to questions posed by the researcher. This type of interaction becomes more valuable as more surveys are filled out and users offer their perspectives on the issues.

Generally, analysis of this type requires a systematic approach with a spreadsheet and sorting routine, and regular reports concluding with a final report after the end date of the collection period. Links to the online survey are generally posted on a variety of communications channels to the stakeholder groups. Technology considerations and cultural sensitivities may be at play and so there is typically a hardcopy method also available. However, because questions may deal with values based perspectives or culturally sensitive material, using surveys on their own risks yielding erroneous results. Focus groups can help make the people connection, and form deeper relationships.

Social media tools like instant messaging and instantaneous feedback methods are limited to one-to-one communications but work well

127

with smaller groups of stakeholders who are already involved. Introductory information and questions can usually be answered with a CSR engagement document. This provides a level of service that no other communications channel other than direct line can provide. Nothing can replace face-to-face meetings. However, with the power of net meetings, video conferencing and online presentations, you can save time and carbon from unnecessary travel and alleviate employees and stakeholders of juggling meeting times thus allowing for greater participation. Another advantage of net meetings is the ability to do instant online polls, creating feedback on the fly and revealing the feedback in a graphical form for discussion. Regardless, try to have real face time with stakeholders when possible - email is great for information sake, yet poor for communication.

Social media tools should not be underestimated. Students, associations and unions have all taken to creating domains and blogs to unite people on a common effort. Even the President of the United States of America, Barrack Obama, used social networking online that was said to have been a major determinant of the success of communicating his platform. On political fronts, online networking has been used to relay information and photos from places typically under despot conditions or under information blackout to communities around the world. Online *YouTube* videos and media have been used in courts of law and to unite families around the globe. It can be powerful stuff if understood and done properly.

In choosing or qualifying a stakeholder, there will surface a list of questions or requirements that will sort out your preliminary list. Some questions to ask:

- Does the stakeholders have an ability to influence the firm's behaviour or outcomes?
- What is the nature of the stakeholder's relationship?
- Is the firm dependent on a dominant stakeholder or is the firm significantly responsible for the stakeholder's wellbeing?
- What is a risk with both the stakeholder and the firm or what is the form of the investment that binds the two?

- Are there outstanding claims for legal rights, assets or property that may affect moral claims?
- Is there a contractual obligation or legitimate claim expressed?
- What is the urgency of the claims or issues?

Throughout the process of evaluating the stakeholder perspectives, needs and interests, various capabilities and faults will surface in what you can and cannot do. The organization will necessarily go through the same process from the stakeholder perspective. Start preparing a SWOT analysis. The opportunities and threats should be noted on an individual and team basis to perform an alignment of capabilities, skills and experience when developing the strategy or program and also to not undermine rapport by ignoring or avoiding suggestions that may seem critical of the organization.

There is some merit in doing a SWOT analysis. The strengths and weaknesses are introspective to the organization, while the opportunities and threats are looking at the external stakeholders and environmental conditions. Factors are defined by people, rules, norms of behaviour, image and market conditions. This is also an opportunity to 'SWOT' the social and environmental position of the organization before embarking on a reconfiguration or the formulation of a CSR or corporate affairs team.

Developing Indicators and Metrics

Indicator measurement is crucial to managing organizational performance. It begins with a sincere appeal to co-create a new vision and in choosing on what is important to focus.

Developing indicators also sets the basis for the reporting of the non-financial performance of the business. We mentioned information gathering techniques and the importance of measuring progress earlier. Now it's time to put information to good use and translate it into strategy and action and a decision support system. Indicators will allow us to monitor our actions against our desired outcomes, assess impacts of decisions and investments, and align business resources for greater performance and co-benefit.

129

Developing indicators for non-financial performance is different to adopting a set list of accounting standards. Total Cost Assessment (TCA) and Total Quality Environmental Management (TQEM) are ways a business can improve their bottom line, especially in the realm of waste management and pollution. This is because minimizing or avoiding waste generating activities is a more cost effective approach than the traditional 'end-of-pipe' strategies (Curkovic & Sroufe, 2006). TQEM is a proactive approach to replacing the traditional waste generating streams of activities. Recognizing that any waste equals lost revenue means that employing a TQEM program has rewards economically, socially and environmentally.

Managers may have difficulty supporting TQEM investments and adopting TQEM methods because of the lack of experience in developing a performance measure system. Evaluation is a key aspect of any program and feedback is essential to fine-tuning adaptive strategies. First, companies must commit and incorporate TQEM into the capital budgeting process to improve decision-making capacity. TQEM enhancements to capacity include the consideration of environmental alternatives to traditional non-environmental projects for capital budget allocation. TCA comes into play when examining existing environmental costs for the business. This includes direct and indirect cost analysis to products, processes, and services. Opportunities may also be found in different areas of business:

- Research and development
- Design
- Manufacturing
- Marketing
- Sales

All the costs that go into a process must be uncovered and accounted for. Inefficient allocation decisions may have hidden environmental costs or accounted for them in a general overhead category making it difficult to recognize as an opportunity for improvement. Thus developing a cost-benefit inventory will be essential to the financial analysis of any TQEM project. Curkovic & Sroufe (2006) recommend breaking down the analysis into 'Four Tiers' in order to recognize all the costs:

- **Direct costs** associated with the product, process or service. Look for data in capital expenditures, equipment installation, project engineering, material, labour and waste management

- **Hidden costs** in areas such as regulation and compliance. A list of regulations and laws must be listed and compliance costs stated now and in the future. May include compliance reporting, education and training, legal support, field testing and sampling costs

- **Contingent liability costs** include accidents, legal damages, settlements or personal injury. These may be estimated based on past experience or examining case studies of other businesses within the same industry

- **Less tangible costs** are not easily denoted. These could include benefits such as higher productivity from increased employee satisfaction, community involvement, improved public relations. Costs could include negative corporate image, stressed relationships with stakeholders, poor transparency and communications because of the poor performance.

Once the total benefits and costs are accounted for, metrics and strategy for improved performance can be designed.

Metrics are usually derived through the stakeholder process and complex negotiations with custom compliance rules. The development of indicators may be related to adopting a widespread standard or code, which may be due to market competition or compliance. Whatever the outcome, the indicators must be reliable and valid to the goals to be useful.

The reliability of information brings consistency to information gathering. For example, collecting a survey from the workplace will yield many different answers to the questions depending on everything from gender to department configuration. In this case the answers will tell us little and have little correlation. The quality of the information will depend on the organization coordinating and communicating the survey for the purposes of either designing the CSR program or developing the system of metrics. Surveys delivered haphazardly will not reveal the organization profile in employment rights and opportunities or environmental hazards. Management and employees can often have disparate views on workplace dynamics. Consider using group sessions led by a third party and a discovery process for discerning opportunities and barriers to developing organizational metrics.

The validity of metrics brings relevance and importance to the process and ensures that that matters and outcomes that are important to stakeholders are accurately measured. It may be that the easiest metrics to report are not the most informative. A firm may focus on what it can do and report most easily to show progress but may continue doing harm in ways that are difficult to monitor. This presents a significant challenge to developing a meaningful set of indicators and measuring non-financial performance.

Validity of information also includes the supply chain operations. A firm may sell off its most polluting assets and lower its footprint, but may encourage greater damage in obtaining its means for production and service. Ignoring a supplier's performance does not necessarily improve overall welfare. Validity also speaks to the stakeholder's values and beliefs. Through the stakeholder process, you will obtain and reveal what is truly important to them as members of business, community and society – none of these areas of life and business are mutually exclusive.

Metrics on their own have little value to groups. It's preferable to translate and communicate findings in a way that everyone can come to understand and make conclusions that are actionable. This is the difference between printing out a cryptic spreadsheet that only a forensic accountant can decipher, or a graphical analysis with summary points that can speak to every level of stakeholder.

Communicating the metrics is the hub of the CSR report and begins the process of brainstorming, innovation and partnerships for a continuous improvement cycle. The value of a good non-financial report is a springboard for being recognized for industry awards, communicating to new and potential partners and creating market share. It is important that the company report on the plans and actions related to meeting the objectives of the CSR even if the indicators appear stagnant. The value of transparency speaks volumes to partners and clients. This is why companies that have no CSR at all remain suspect and are ever becoming the dark horse of industry and a detractor for talent.

When we plan for sustainability, we need to do a holistic inspection of various systems. The indicators that arise will become markers of progress and reflect priorities in the areas of economy, society and environment.

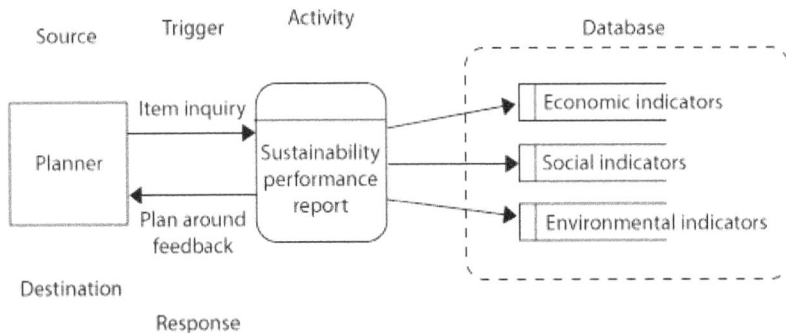

Deriving indicators need not be numerous nor complex, but be must be understood and have the ability to alter policy and create actionable tasks. In fact, it is best to keep indicators to a manageable level as the complexity and energy required for gathering input and disseminating the activities grows with each observation.

The International Institute for Sustainable Development (www.iisd.org) defines the evolution of corporate progress reporting from one-off environmental reports to full-production print and online linkages between organization and social and environmental linkages. The report, whether produced annually or more frequently is the end result of the work done to create productivity and balance in the three

133

areas of economic, social and environment progress. A concise report reflecting current events and examining future trends is necessary to update members and employees with the proper intelligence information. Traditional economic forecasting is becoming increasingly unreliable in a world of change that is pushing out traditional economic cycles (Davis & Blass, 2007). Communicating information and extrapolating trends based on certainties of the past will create less effective behaviours for future performance.

Recent studies suggest that companies are poorly communicating their CSR activities to the external stakeholders and in some case to the internal stakeholders. The firm is wasting resources and losing social capital that could otherwise translate to increased brand recognition and long term benefits. Communications goals should include increased awareness and reduced scepticism by strategizing what to communicate and where to communicate and knowing which factors are most relevant to stakeholders. Many firms may have decided their CSR agendas but their communications and engagement strategies can always be improved or aligned to assist CSR objectives.

The critical part in the cycle of stakeholder engagement and information processing is the final reporting aspect. Data must be made meaningful, assembled and formatted into packages that are usable by managers and decision makers (Berc et al., 1998). The CSR planner essentially acts as an organizational manager to gather, interpret and disseminate information to create organizational change for effectiveness and better performance.

Figure 18. Information role of structural characteristics for reducing equivocality or uncertainty (Daft & Lengel, 1986, p. 561).

| Rules and Regulations | Formal Information System | Special Reports | Planning | Direct contact | Integrator | Group Meetings |

Equivocality reduction
(Clarify, reach agreement
decide which questions to ask)

Uncertainty reduction
(Obtain additional data, seek
answers to explicit questions)

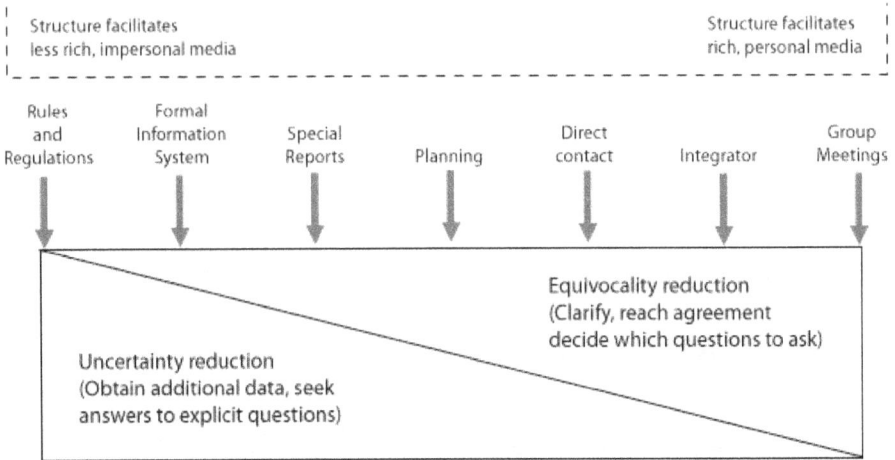

Strict reliance on technology and information can create an "attention deficit disorder" (ADD) as it consumes the attention of the recipient. "Organizational ADD results in increased chances of missing key information, a lack of focus, and an inability to hold another's attention." (Desouza & Hensgen, 2005, p. 133). The use of communications media and personal contact provides a more effective means of communicating, reducing ambiguity and uncertainty – a goal of systems thinking. Looking at the attached image for the structural characteristics of information exchange, we can see how bringing in the interpersonal aspect shifts the uncertainty quotient from one end of the spectrum to the other. You can maintain a balanced communications plan that includes media and people.

Use of media channels may highlight a company's success but may not communicate a corporate strategy or framework to its CSR stakeholders in that particular medium. This can be perceived as a lack of social sensitivity and may waste time, money and effort on all sides. Using mixed media is a great way to create a multi-sensory and dual-hemisphere approach to delivering comprehension. Delivering an effective message is more important then repetition. One creates motivation and buy-in, the other, memorization. A real understanding of a firm's need to integrate social and environmental concerns will communicate much more clearly and will influence operations in a positive manner. The ultimate goal is to alter the organizational belief system in terms of what is possible and practical.

135

Psst! Spread The Word

Social marketing (SM) is the internal medium for communicating ways for individuals and groups to reach goals in health, sustainability and community improvement. These types of campaigns can be successful in altering people's awareness and habits while growing the business. As critical mass and tipping points are reached, whole communities can reap the benefits of adopting or recognizing a superior quality product or service in economic, social, and environmental performance. The business bottom-line benefits from acknowledging and forecasting social trends and having a complimentary CSR to help drive the strategy. Disseminating the positive message through the informal culture of the organization is more effective than releasing a memo.

It is important not to confuse social marketing with commercial marketing. While the goal of generic marketing is to sell a product, create exchange and improve shareholder returns, social marketing involves the firm's stakeholders and clients and seeks to improve the overall quality of life. These are long-term strategies and relationship development techniques, not one-off campaigns.

Although SM uses commercial marketing theories, tools and techniques to market for progress in social issues, social marketers have more difficult goals: to make potentially difficult and long-term behavioural change in target populations. The goals are usually wide-ranging and apply to most of the population (i.e. health initiatives, recycling, etc.). Because of its societal applications, social marketing often markets to government, NGOs, and citizen alliance groups. These realities informed Lazer and Kelly's original definition of social marketing: "Social marketing is concerned with the application of marketing knowledge, concepts, and techniques to enhance social as well as economic ends. It is also concerned with the analysis of the social consequences of marketing policies, decisions and activities."

Social Marketing has an exceptional focus on using tools that build relationships. Like conventional marketing, it starts and finishes with research, and research is conducted continuously to inform the development of the strategy. A situational analysis of the internal and external environment and the profile of the consumer or stakeholder is conducted first. This assists in the segmentation of the market and defines the targeting strategy. Business objectives are revisited and redefined align objectives for the programme and to inform the formulation of the marketing strategy. The elements of the social marketing mix are then developed and pre-tested, before being implemented. Finally, the relative success of the plan is monitored and the outcome evaluated.

Just as stakeholders may never fully understand the firm's competitive strategy, capabilities or the trade-offs it has to make, the firm must understand its impacts and opportunities with various stakeholder groups. In this way, the business does not attempt to understand why the client is not participating, but rather looks internally to understand why the organization does not understand its target market. Once the dynamics of the internal marketing campaign are understood, a more relevant and successful campaign can be launched to external stakeholders.

Public relations is key to obtaining stakeholder buy-in, but long gone are the days when a persuasive media campaign sways peoples beliefs. An organization must not confuse its social and business results with its public relations campaign.

CSR messages that are strictly about social issues are viewed suspiciously as they don't fit with historical advertising. Unless the social issue is not a ploy in self-interest, consumers will view the message as an ulterior motive. Generally, CSR messages are about direct involvement in a social issue and can communicate the commitment, why it chooses this particular cause (motives), the impacts it is having on the issue, and articulate the fit between organization and the cause (Shuili et al.).

You may be responsible for developing and supporting your organization's CSR program or you may be an external stakeholder and be seeking to market your initiatives to gain funding and support. Either way there are approaches to winning corporate buy-in.

137

Select the key issues under your mandate that would most benefit from additional resources. You may find a connection with corporations and communities that relates to their mission, values or desire for improvement in a particular area. Highlight interests in common and communicate the logic and passion for the issues. Don't be afraid to ask for feedback. Find out what is most important to them and share stories of success and other communities where connections were made.

When preparing a proposal to engage a business, present several initiatives for support that best match their business and marketing needs. Know the business and know your material, then sell your strengths, resources and potential partners that you bring to enhance the deal. List any endorsements or get new ones that would help. Pitch all the benefits and develop a marketing program that shows this understanding and that shows your own commitment to implementing, carrying the administrative load, preparing reports and recognize the company contribution in ways that are preferred by the company.

Inside Innovation

Innovation is a forgotten art, relegated as an epiphany left to artists, designers and inventors who convey images of working out of their basements or garage. The last 100 years of business management has focused on, for the most part, automation, mechanization and the 'routine-ization' of work. Where did the creativity go ... to the marketing department for approval? The reinforcement of status quo has produced an aversion to the creative risk-taking needed to breakthrough the muck.

Reliance on technology to produce progress in business and society has had mixed results. We enjoy the communications benefits but at the cost of constant upgrading, distraction, and a tremendous amount of toxic waste. We end up talking or meeting more but taking less action on things that really matter.

Communication that lacks impact leading to a positive action is not communication at all. Innovation looks to use technology as a tool to produce a game-changer – creative disruption. It can be a personal change in one's life that creates a breakthrough in skills or attitude or an organizational change that sets a new direction for a responsible and enthusiastic institution focused on doing good.

'We cannot solve the world's problems with the same mind that created them', to paraphrase Albert Einstein, means we must learn from experiences and adapt to create something new. Innovation allows us to survive and prosper, but how do we move forward when the status quo is so deeply entrenched in our economic, social and environmental systems and organizational structures?

To innovate requires us to desire and strive for excellence – excellence meaning something better. A combination of higher motives that include both material and spiritual ideals in the spirit of cooperation will build the trust and allow for a forum of social exchange. Striving for excellence is driven by motivation and is entirely voluntary in contrast to the command and conquer compliance organization.

In his search for what defines excellence in a human, Aristotle offered insights more suited to a model for organizations where cooperation was the norm (Nahapiet et al., 2005). These insights still ring true in discerning those values that bring excellence in organizational behaviour. Nahapiet, Gratton and Rocha extract four tenets that show how a social and relational model can be learned and developed:

Tenet 1: Striving for excellence

In contrast to the self-interest motivation model that suggests all humans are motivated by wealth, power and materials good, Aristotle proposes that humans are driven by a quest for excellence. Human intentionality is based on an aspiration to meld material gain with duty and sentiment, valuing equally goods, friendship and virtues.

Tenet 2: An integration of self and others

139

Individuals are at the same time independent and social and thus other people's interests are important and just as legitimate. Interaction with others is viewed as a means to achieve mutual goals, enhancing the relationship. Interaction allows for feedback, review, dialogue, greater critical analysis and improved social relations.

Tenet 3: The habits of cooperation

Aristotle believed that all people possess intelligence and free will to pursue truth and what is good about themselves. Developing intelligence and the pursuit of truth requires work and thus requires one to be consistently responsible through training and repetition. Cooperation also needs to be worked at and consistently engaged.

Tenet 4: Philia: The importance of relationships

Relationships must be mutual and recognized as being based on goodwill. This will inherently lead to cooperation. A traditional hierarchy, or 'top-down' approach, will task members based on compliance not commitment. Opening the dialogue from the bottom up will reflect the importance of the relationship amongst members with management.

The four tenets described above reveal the importance of the strength of positive social relations in achieving excellence.

Using strategy and leadership we can create the capacity for change by forecasting and anticipating, employing vision exercises, being flexible, and working with others to mutual benefit. The good design of work roles and responsibilities can encourage individuals to strive for excellence provided tasks challenge them to grow and flourish using their talents. However, obtaining excellence goes beyond job design as motivations are tied to a life of meaning, the joy of relationships and satisfaction in one's work. It is about the engaging the whole person and spirit, not just some part of them.

To make intellectual and moral progress, the notion of status quo must be absolved. The Lewin's model used here again, frames how an organization breaks old behaviours and adopts new ones, and gives us a basic encapsulation to embracing change. It is a transitional model that represents the organizational, cultural and psychological change that must occur. Much like a grievance, the status quo mentality will resist change as it represents insecurity and risk.

By changing the equilibrium between the opposing forces of the status quo and transformation, managers can affect change by exerting pressure in one direction. Here is another look at Lewin's model as a reminder:

Lewin's change management model

Status Quo — Unfreeze — Forces — Change — Re-freeze

First, the organization must 'unfreeze' itself from the status quo, whether rewards are taken away for current behaviour or demerits given for not adopting new ones. Old assumptions must be challenged, as there is never 'a single right way to do things' in a continuous learning and adaptive environment. Allow for the creative disruption to breath freely.

During times of great transition, options must be available for training and education for employees, to help guide them into the new vision. There is a tension that will be created as survival anxiety and learning anxiety rise and are challenged by the imposition of new ideas and methods. Use creative and interactive group sessions that support the positive aspects of the change and consistently reinforce the vision to provide more security and overcome learning anxiety.

In the change phase, identify champions and communicate new concepts, meanings and standards. Bring examples to life by showing what others have done and the positive results they have had. Doubt will always exist because uncertainty is simply the reality. Openly discuss the best ways to improve the learning process, but be aware of tactics from individuals to fall into old behaviours that include denial, scapegoating or bargaining.

141

Finally, the organization must 're-freeze' the new behaviours and ensure alignment with the new vision. If people are not sure of their new roles or cannot be delegated responsibilities to be carried out, look for an unfinished change management initiative. Communication may not have been as consistent and clear as is needed during a time of change. In this case, re-align and communicate roles with clarity and offer support for additional training.

The new culture should foster an open environment that is supportive of expression and networking for greater knowledge transfer. Engendering creativity is vital to innovation success. Creating the organizational environment for innovation is neither disruptive nor expensive. In fact, a firm does not even need to institute an innovation program provided it meets four criteria, regardless of size, industry or financial resources (Rosa, Qualis, & Fuentes, 2008, p. 631).

1. Manage organizations so that their knowledge base is more diverse than would occur naturally.
2. Encourage employees to embrace a collaborative and non-complacent attitude towards work and the organization.
3. Make it possible for organization members to engage in the quick testing of ideas and solutions as they emerge.
4. Reward employee and supervisor behaviours that support these principles and punish resistance to their implementation.

Consultant Gary Hamel has coined the term 'wheel of innovation', which involves these five steps:

1. Imagining
2. Designing
3. Experimenting
4. Assessing
5. Scaling

New ideas must be relevant and be well implemented to improve the organization. Peter Drucker points out "Successful organizations...are now being turned out by cross-functional teams with people from marketing, manufacturing, and finance participating in research work from the beginning".

Supporting innovation also requires the following roles to be filled across an inter-disciplinary team:

Idea generators - people who create insights and awareness
Information gatekeepers - people who connect and link others
Product champions - people who uptake and champion new causes
Project managers - technical functions and tracking
Innovation leaders - people who encourage and maintain the values and momentum

It is management's responsibility to recognize the spectrum of abilities and to identify and fulfil the various roles of an innovation team. Creativity can be fostered through free dialogue and free action that demonstrates support for the learning environment.

So, go ahead and create a learning environment. Change requires courage while fear stifles. Ensure actual physical space to use a whiteboard, draw, scream and meditate – a place purely for creative interaction. People can only challenge themselves and feel that their skills are of use when they can be applied to an initiative that motivates them to participate. Allowing the free flow of knowledge and interaction will create a critical mass of ideas and collaboration that will be based on outcomes that benefit the whole of the organization.

Innovation is more a product of social capital than leadership. The spread of information and the number of connections in a network is a greater influence on the adoption of an idea or product than persuasion (Delre, Jager, Bijmolt, & Janssen, 2010). If we factor in individual values, a well-communicated CSR program should increase both client and consumer adoption of an organizational initiative, product or service. The leadership role is crucial to obtaining a balance in power and influence and in so doing, innovation.

A Growing Consciousness

Traditional management science emphasizes behaviour and economic value and as a result has omitted the human component for more transcendent meaning in one's own work. People bring more to work than their brains and bodies. There is creativity, intention, and an innate desire for personal progress on many levels that a workplace does not address. For many, the workplace is an oppressive organizational structure in which people repress their best abilities and dedicate themselves through obligation rather than through internal motivation. Sometimes – perhaps mostly - monetary rewards alone are not enough for wellbeing.

In times of stress and in need to relieve oneself of the monotony of a workplace, people seek re-creation or exercise. Physical activity is important for health, so is mental balance. The need for meditational practice or reflection becomes greater in difficult times. The huge popularity in yoga has spurred a new health industry. Health and spirituality is not only good for one's self, it's good for business.

We spend the most productive hours of our conscious life performing tasks, sometimes routine, sometimes redundant, at times challenging. It is during those times when we are free to think, deliberate, challenge and move autonomously that genius may arise. In psychology, a schema is a fixed neural framework, reinforced typically from a trauma and an inability to cope. A workplace may trigger negative schemas, reducing self-esteem and self-worth. In times of self-reflection, people may deem themselves of little value if not recognized by peers and supervisors for their positive attributes. Relieving the division created by the neglect of our higher potential is key to productivity, health and cultural change.

Some corporations insist that you 'leave your values at the door' when working. This duality is harmful to employee satisfaction and belonging, as well as painting an unrealistic picture of the reality of work impacts and community integration. Understanding workplace culture, influences and social and environmental impacts is no longer the purview of the human resources department but for all managers in the organization. As the world quickly changes we need to change with it, and this will affect the structure and function of the traditional workplace. CSR can become a consciousness-raising experience and bring back into the fold human values and positive attitudes towards each other, and towards nature that has served through the history of mankind.

Let's try stopping the need to put everything into boxes. The modern workplace is typically a leased or owned building, which is then filled with stuff from furniture and electronics. The expectation is that people will come to this 'place' and perform great work inside this box. Going to work for some is the equivalent of daytime house arrest. Creating 'freedom' spaces in and around the workplace allows for expression and collaboration. Having space for finding peace is equally important. Do we think it a coincidence that Google offices have meditation rooms and place for employees to roam in a 'campus' setting?

To be creative or to apply problem-solving skills, stretches of uninterrupted time may be required. Going beyond CSR will mean acknowledging the need to be creative and productive, and ensuring that the culture and environment foster these most important attributes.

In the words of Jason Fried – 'would you expect to have a good night's sleep if you were constantly interrupted?' – so why is it not the same for workflow? Jason brings it down to two elements: Managers and Meetings. Managers do not do the work for you but check into the work you are doing which is an interruption. Meetings can be the most toxic, unproductive and expensive elements in an organization and need to be reformatted to allow for creativity and reduced interruption. You will find that these traditional and archaic practices to improving workspace will need to change to meet with the social and practical realities of doing good work.

Looking at Hart and Milstein's Sustainable Value Framework, a firm can examine its practices through different business lenses and provide value to shareholders and stakeholders.

145

The future workplace will require leadership with a real sustainable vision, a workplace culture that is open and innovative, and a renewed ethic that incorporates the client and communities, looking beyond the traditional materialism that has driven the industrial age.

The New Leadership

Leadership in the future workplace will have dramatically different characteristics and skills than have traditionally existed. The new leader will not be the widget counting daemon of yesteryear, but a social systems designer. They will work with teams of people to manifest their internal motivational factors to higher more meaningful goals. The leader as teacher will create autonomous responsibility and allow creativity enough for individuals to develop their higher selves – a building of social capital.

A leader that exudes integrity sustains the organization. A leader that is popular can persuade and capture the imagination and energy of the entire company and beyond into the communities in which it serves. It is important that a leader understand what it means to be in service of those they are leading and how to motivate them to achieve higher ambitions both individually and as a group. Building an effective organization has less to do with focusing on organizational structure and systems than emphasizing people, purpose, and process (Pastoriza et al., 2009, p. 485).

With the requirement for a business to innovate to survive, leadership must assure that a learning organizational model is applied. Organizational learning is a primary source of competitive advantage. Where bureaucracies focus on doing what's right, performance based organization focus on doing the right things, and learning organizations create the capacity to do both better (Amy, 2008).

When leading a group, there are unspoken expectations in both behaviour and direction that are communicated from the leader. There are also many other functions that a leader can execute that bring intrinsic and intangible benefits to the organization; this one is difficult because the group themselves may not be aware that these

146

functions exist at all. For example, motivation cannot be ordered or instructed as a function to perform, it is an adopted attitude that leads to enhanced behaviour that benefits the individual and company.

First we need to look at the basics of motivation of which, some concepts will derive from psychology, sociology, anthropology, and administrative sciences or management principles. From the business side, an organization typically has a human resource function that assumes the roles of attracting and nurturing talent. Businesses typically do not have dynamic approach to every type of individual needs and thus do not actually support the employee role as much as they support the organization. By attempting to make the people fit into the grand design of the organizational structure they lose the potential. Combine the lack of psychology, training, experimental models, diversity and culture awareness, and external influences and HR departments are reduced to the application of benefits, hiring and firing.

The quality of leadership communication is a key indicator of the quality of management. Words only account for seven per cent of all communication between people and actions speak louder than words. A competent communicator possesses some of the following characteristics:

- The ability to choose from a wide range of actions
- The ability to choose the most appropriate behaviour
- The skill at performing behaviours
- The ability to be empathic and see other perspectives
- The ability to view an issue from multiple frames of reference
- The ability to objectively perform self-monitoring or self-observation (Adler & Rodman, 1997)

Change leadership will require making different choices and those choices must be informed from a new array of information, know-how and purpose. Change will also mean having the courage to let go of status quo mentality, and developing a positive motivational message to create new behaviours. Increasingly, companies have put the onus for continuous learning, developing new skills, and personal advancement, on the individual. Thus, there are no longer careers within a company but transience across many types of businesses and functions to reach those personal and professional milestones that a company has omitted.

Leaders must demonstrate the interpersonal skills, problem solving and vision necessary to the job. A leader's personal values and disposition will play a greater role in the future, as members of organizations want to know how they are aligned with the governance of the organization structure.

Surveys reflect that functional and expert skills are not as good people skills, ethics and nature of the workplace. With trends of paperless and mobile operations, leaders who can manage the evolution of an organization where profit focus, targets, and strict rules will become less important will be in demand. Who would you rather follow and work for - a leader that generates profit at everyone's expense, or someone who can build a sustainable organization that understands employee wellbeing? Which do you think will perform better in the long run?

Globalization and virtualization has created business dynamics that include a temporal dimension. Managers will need to understand the dynamics of managing an organization across space and time, with relationships that are more complex than traditional structures could encompass. A real leader will balance the security and predictability of a bureaucracy with the flexibility of the new age lifestyles that come with virtualization.

Ann David and Eddie Blass (2007) conducted a survey to former MBA graduates about the future of the workplace and discovered prevalent themes throughout the response stream. Among the changes that were expected were:

- A move away from the 'company worker' to a more autonomous, flexible, responsive and widely skilled professional
- Control systems will be loosened and less bureaucratic, reducing politics at work

- Accommodation of life perspectives
- Work will be more fun

Structure was among the top reasons for a 'bad' organization. A workplace that is overly structured appears to produce greater stress responses. Many of the respondents also used words such as greedy, unhappy and selfish to describe the modern workplace. Although flexibility and autonomy were highly desirable, a sense of membership and belonging was important to not feel isolated in one's work.

Going beyond CSR to include the development of a flexible cohesive workplace where the individual is valued for their views and personal contributions to the organizational strategy is necessary for a positive workspace.

'Out with the old, in with the new'

The transformational leader is needed in the new economy, to lead the organization with an understanding of the complexity and motivation that is needed to succeed in business and environmental protection. Only a leader with wisdom and understanding can tap into people's psyche, their cores. It is that same passion that Martin Luther King Jr. exuded. He tapped into the heart of the matter and into the soul of the people with a passion that resonates even today.

A leader is a person that will be defined by their ability to use social exchange in clarifying goals and expectations, and provide a clear path to rewards for achievement. Such leaders will inspire and share their vision, empower the organization members to achieve that vision and provide resources to allow members to reach their full potential by underscoring the ultimate purpose of their roles in the organization. Characteristics and behaviours of transformational leaders include charisma, vision, and the ability to inspire. Leaders must be seen as credible, not cheerleaders with an empty message, but an intellectual challenge with credibility.

A good leader's reasoning is sound and backed by knowledge of the product or process, expressing all the benefits of continuous evolution

149

derived from a long-term vision. The leader's stories resonate with the lives of everyone in the audience and agreement for a new direction is obtained by establishing common ground. There is also a one-on-one transaction that results in greater commitment to the mission and to teach people to think in new ways and evolve into knowledge workers. This usually means challenging long-held traditions. Real leadership establishes a new way of being, acting in a servant leadership position by putting the interests of the followers before their own, focusing on personal growth and empowerment for the organization as a whole.

Managers must be able to see the results of their emotional and participative investment in their organization. The feedback from workers and followers is important and associated metrics such as wellbeing indicators will provide direction and adaptive management for continued and renewed efforts at improvements. Managers have the capacity to hold a shared vision with the rest of the organization. Leadership is not about selling an idea like CSR or convincing people to change. It's about an emotional connection driven by a unanimous quest for higher meaning in the business relationship.

"An invasion of an army can be resisted, but not an idea whose time has come" - Victor Hugo

In redefining an organization, a leader must redefine the thinking that reinforces its structure and process. This has much to do with entrenched beliefs and world views and applications of knowledge management. Leading into a responsible organization requires the knowledge base of the business ecosystem and understanding the inputs and impacts of the business. How many bad business decisions are being made, affecting numbers of people every day, from either ignorance or lack of understanding? How much money and resources could have been saved over the long-run if there were another avenue for gathering input? These questions need to be consistently asked and explored.

But it is not enough to ask questions and get answers. There are answers that require action and there are answers that require questions. A leader's work is established by getting things done through others, this is why charisma and emotional intelligence are important traits - to motivate others to perform beyond the communications and exceed expectations. This lets employees interpret for themselves the intangibles of the message. The quality and attitude of the perception will be derived from how they feel about the messenger and the organization. This is how a superior product or service arises, through self-actualization of employees who use their talents to discern what is best.

The leader thinks in systems, and will elucidate the connections and relationships that are part of the decision making process. Systems thinking is not just a tool for identifying stakeholders but for forecasting the social and environmental impacts of those same decisions. Decisions may be fraught with politics, personal translation, and institutional history but these are not important. Allowing corporate politics to influence decisions can possibly be the least productive way to get things done (*Harvard business review on the persuasive leader*, 2008). The *Inquiry* process is suggested by David Garvin and Michael Roberto as the more powerful method to make decisions. The inquiry process requires careful attention to three factors:

1. fostering constructive conflict (as opposed to personal);
2. accepting and confirming the consideration of all viewpoints even if not ultimately accepted;
3. and knowing when to close deliberations (or more easily - conflict, consideration, closure)

How many times have you been to a meeting and seen few options on the table for progress? This neither permits active involvement in the organization or sufficient evaluation of options to make the best choice. In fact, Garvin and Roberto' research over several years suggests leaders get decision making all wrong. Decisions are consistently treated as a singular event rather than an integrated process. They might mull over those demonic spreadsheets and bullet points, pay heed to their gut instincts and still overlook the social and organizational factors that could ultimately undermine success. Good leaders understand that decisions are not solo events and instruments

151

of control, they see the systems involved and the processes as a design with many players affecting the quality of the outcome.

Although groups may advocate for a certain position, making cases to win the day or compel people to follow an option leads to the omission of critical information for fear of losing that position. The contestation that can take place leads to a loss of innovation and people fall back into a low-level consciousness about their purpose and direction. The *Inquiry* process is well-suited for establishing or enhancing the direction for a CSR program because of the careful consideration of options. Information flows freely and without bias and critical thinking skills come into play. Conflict may exist in an inquiry debate but it is never personal, always centred on the problem or idea at hand.

The following chart contrasts the approach a leader can take in facilitating group decision-making:

Approaches to Decision-Making		
	Advocacy	**Inquiry**
Concept of decision-making	A contest	Collaborative problem solving
Purpose of discussion	Persuasion and lobbying	Testing and evaluation
Participants' role	Spokespeople	Critical thinkers
Patterns of Behaviour	Strive to persuade others Defend your position Downplay weaknesses	Present balanced arguments Remain open to alternatives Accept constructive criticism
Minority views	Discouraged or dismissed	Cultivated and valued
Outcome	Winners and losers	Collective ownership
(*Harvard business review on the persuasive leader*, 2008, p. 148)		

Conflict may also arise when there are 'inquirers' and 'advocates' in the same room. Inquiring types will often argue for a more thorough approach and question the mainstream thinking if the logic is not complete. Advocates need to win their position as spokespeople for their cause. As a leader looking for a progressive collaborative method, advocates must be recognized but streamed to a team-building environment to get everyone on-side. This could mean change that employees were not anticipating.

When people become members of a group, be it a community or organization, they automatically subscribe to the influence and values of that group. Not doing so would find them in exclusionary territory. That influence translates to internal thoughts that draw and map our picture of the external world. Our thoughts only make sense in the context of the cultural background within which we are subscribed. In any organization, there is a formal culture and an informal culture. The cultural background gives meaning and context to individual thoughts, thoughts that would not exist if one did not belong to a community of individuals who also interact and share thoughts. Thus, the cultural community serves as the background and context for driving thoughts, perspective and values (Wilber, 1997).

Without cultural symbols, language, practices, one might not have thoughts of any meaning at all. But culture does not exist as an immaterial function: it expresses itself in social production. The material components of technology - agriculture, industry, codes, politics - are all part of the social system that expresses a particular worldview. Ken Wilber's describes four domains for consideration that drive our views of the world – intentional, behavioural, cultural and social. The internal processes belong to the 'I' or 'we' domains of intention (singular) and culture (group) and the external process 'it' represented by our behaviour (singular) and our social systems (group).

When we look at how people seek to integrate their thoughts and lives into their environments with others, Wilber's methods explain consciousness on a much deeper and integrative level than does traditional organizational behaviour or conflict resolution management. This explanation enhances our understanding of how people truly feel and behave in their lives than does traditional organizational behaviour. People strive to align their thoughts with the cultural backdrop of the setting they subscribe to. In a place of employment, this is no difference. Thus a culture of sustainability in an organization will yield thoughts, behaviours and social groups based on the culture.

Humans are natural seekers of truth and knowledge, especially when it comes to health, history, and spirituality. When our internal thoughts and beliefs conflict with our external environment, we have cognitive dissonance, which causes individual stress and weakens the group network of which they are a part. How can someone who cares about the health of their family knowingly work for an organization that is creating a harmful toxic by-product? The CSR program should be based on the true perspectives of the organization's members and integrate to a point where it influences a culture of responsibility and innovation from the individual to the social systems. It may be best to break the program in into five perspectives:

1) material; 2) body; 3) mind; 4) soul; and 5) spirit.

These five perspectives will address the external physical resource planning, the human interaction with those resources, the logic behind the program, the individual's own commitment and the values of the group. Ensuring the five perspectives are aligned will create the cultural cohesion necessary to motivate and innovate.

If we define innovation as the progression of an idea and we premise that there are no absolutely new ideas just evolutions of existing ones, then innovation requires interest or motivation, data or direct experience, and insight or knowledge that can be applied to the existing system. In a tight-knit free flowing information network, communication of the symbols, codes and language occurs with greater quality (or rigor) and sufficient quantity to have a better picture of the external environment from other's perspectives. This is important because our thinking only occurs as a reflection of the group dynamic we associate with.

Also, what we produce as a result or communicate back has a better functional fit with the social systems in place when we assimilate other ideas and perspectives. When this back and forth between members of a group is strong and honest, misinterpretation and risk is reduced and innovation is bound to occur. It may be necessary for managers to step completely out of the organization to bring new insight and attitudes back to the organization. This could include retreats, sabbaticals, or a think tank away from the reaches of the group.

True innovation is enlightenment, it is the moment of eureka and the pro-generator of a series of events that could change many peoples lives. When CSR takes the view of becoming a cultural backdrop for the organization, the hearts and minds of its members will follow. Ensuring the CSR program is built on sincerity, represents the views of its members, is a cultural and structural fit with the group, will result in innovation and be that much more rewarding for all involved.

In the end, building CSR into a business or organization is about building legitimacy. Just as a leader needs to develop perception, harmonize values and follow through to be legitimate, whole organizations are the same. Corporations, governments and societies have fallen because of lack of legitimacy. Reinstitute legitimacy with a fully conscious direction that leads with heart and intelligence, free from the group inertia that promotes stagnancy over movement.

The New Organizational Consciousness

The points within this book inevitably lead to the desire of the creation of the humane workplace. Although much of the material here is academic, that reinforces two points: 1) There is the human dimension that has traditionally become an aversion of managers, caring about the quality of the work and for the people who are a part, and; 2) that humane workplaces for the most part are still theorized and not practised.

When do we fully integrate humanity into our workplaces? Hopefully we have not become so foolish as to leave health and happiness behind in our daily work efforts.

There is enough research and evidence to support the relationship between productivity and happiness. There are also known factors that increase or decrease positive attitudes towards work. Having a good place to work covers more than buildings, parking lots, and cafeteria. In fact, variations on workplace structure built simply for workplace processes had no effect on performance (Baldry & Hallier, 2010). New designs in workspace are more like lifestyles, sharing creative space, inclusive of natural daylight and bio-walls, in house cafes and quiet rooms, which have become the norm for the most desirable places to work. The human component and managerial outlook is critical. If management does not possess the emotional intelligence or faculties to recognize, diagnose and enhance work culture and performance, both in structure and culture, then they are in the wrong job and should probably cease making others miserable.

The popularity for green buildings and healthy work interiors is driving talent to those workplaces that can bring 'fun' and health into work. Companies demonstrate what they value. Either employees come first or profit, however I can find no evidence to suggest that one sacrifices the other. If the path to success in life means optimum health, a positive outlook, pristine quality of environment and rewarding relationships, what makes financial success any different? A long-term study conducted by Columbia University, led by David Lewin, covered 495 organizations, and included collaborating partners Alfred P. Sloan Foundation, Carnegie Mellon University, and The World Bank, concluded the following:

- Companies that share profits with employees have significantly better financial performance than those that don't
- Companies that share information and engage their employees perform significantly better than autocratic firms
- Flexible work design is significantly related to success
- Training and development have a positive effect on financial performance
- Two-thirds of the bottom line impact was a result of the combination of the above factors

Applying these humanistic practices don't impact only the bottom-line but actually helps to cause it (Maslow, Stephens, Heil, & Maslow, 1998, pp. 51-52). It follows that a profit-oriented workplace that looks only at the bottom line will reinforce a workplace that is based on efficiency, stuffing humans into ever smaller spaces, reducing privacy and dignity to support rules of process. A bureaucratic organization bent on mechanizing human qualities is already a failure. The outsides of buildings promote the power and brand of the organization and the inside is designed for running costs - mediocrity at it's finest.

Now imagine what a workplace designed for creating ideas, innovation and sustainable profit would look like. For this creativity to be expressed, the workplace has to reflect the joy and commitment to creating knowledge workers with the right emotional mindset.

Creating the spiritual workplace, in the sense of bringing 'spirit' and the quest for personal excellence, must certainly be the pinnacle of an effective organization. This type of fervent attractiveness has worked for religion, education, and all the largest and most successful clubs and fraternities in the world. Let's take Leo Kim's five points on spiritual doctrines that would imbue the workplace with greater perspective, and the rationale for applying them

1) *We are one with each other and the universe*

This is true from our basic knowledge of physics. We are integrated with our world in unimaginable ways. This perspective reminds us to see in systems and see the big picture better. We would be more environmentally conscious, accepting of other cultures, and better respect our relationships with suppliers, customers and employees. The company image will be more compassionate and empathetic to environmental health and human issues.

2) *The most important ingredients of our world are hidden*

Although Kim remarks on the mystery of life, he also points out that most of our science has yet to be discovered. Essentially acknowledging what we do not know will create anticipation and create drive for exploring our potential.

3) *What we think, we become*

157

Our thoughts have a physiological impact on our brains and bodies, rewiring and recoding our networks at the atomic level. Positive thinking improves health and life. All psychology and spiritual work done, whether its creating through intention, neuro-linguistic programming (NLP), counselling, yoga or meditation is based on our need to achieve contentment and optimal mental health. If a workplace is based on pressure and stress, the most noble attributes of an individual will never be expressed. If anxiety becomes a norm in the workplace, the brain will rewire itself to be anxious and affect output in work and life as a result.

4) *We are not victims of the past and we are empowered to change our lives*

If the work atmosphere is dwelling on what happened and who did what, there can be no progress unless it is an exercise in lesson learned and affirmative action. We can easily accept this principle on the fact that developing a CSR or change program will require getting out of the past and empowering people to create a new future.

5) *There is great power in our collective consciousness*

Imagine the power of everyone voluntarily becoming committed to a single purpose, underscored by a higher ethic, associated with the organization. The combined creative power of a union of minds motivated by the sheer alignment of core values in environment, health, and relationships all driving the new economy would be unstoppable.

Before we jump back into our analytical minds and think it's nonsense, I can highlight a couple of interesting points about the power of consciousness. Medical journals report the positive correlation of thinking positively and reduced mortality – "Both positive affect (e.g., emotional wellbeing, positive mood, joy, happiness, vigour, energy) and positive trait-like dispositions (e.g., life satisfaction, hopefulness, optimism, sense of humour) were associated with reduced mortality in healthy population studies... CONCLUSIONS: The current review suggests that positive psychological wellbeing has a favorable effect on survival in both healthy and diseased populations" (Chida & Steptoe, 2008). This means happy people live healthier more productive lives but that just makes basic sense.

"The idea of the 24x7 workplace which is outsourced to free-lancing portfolio workers is offered in the future workplace in terms of the organization of work, while the current workplace is described by words such as bureaucratic, meritocratic, leaderless, traditional, hierarchical, matrix and results oriented. The future, on the other hand, is described as remote, dispersed, knowledge-led, hybrid and results oriented rather than system focussed. The virtual workplace enabling self-determination and liberation from bureaucracy so beloved of theorists for the past 30 years remains just over the rainbow (Davis & Blass, 2007, p. 44)".

We know through solid research that good social ties are a key component of health. Lack of social cohesion is a major cause of depression. The most consuming and affluent nation is also the most depressed and drugged nation on earth. The National Institute of Mental Health reports in 2008, that over 26% of Americans suffer depression in a given year and is the leading cause of disability for people aged 15-44 in North America. Americans have doubled their uptake of drugs in the last ten years, surpassing the 10 per cent population mark that includes children. Any one of Prozac, Zoloft, Paxil or Celexa, Lexapro or Luvox, Buspar, Nardil, Elavil, Sinequan, Pamelor, Serzone, Desyrel, Norpramin, Tofranil, Adapin, Vivactil, Ludiomil, Endep, Parnate or Remeron qualifies.

I highlight the problems of depression in society as a failure of management to create organizations built on good social practice, health and empowerment. When we spend so much of our waking hours performing for an organization we (are supposed to) believe in, there is an implied responsibility to the group's members as well as from the members to the organization.

Recent studies have shown that a boring job can kill you. Individuals who are not engaged psychically with their work will mentally drift. Job engagement has a direct link to job satisfaction and happiness.

159

When properly organized and free to express spiritually and culturally our connections with life and each other, humans feel whole and supported in their social structures. Economic desires (materialism) and social needs can be balanced for a healthy society to prosper in business, relationships and health.

Successful businesses focus on delivering real value to customers and are able to anticipate and take advantage of rapid change in an increasingly complex environment. As leaders need to quickly adapt, they will become adept at forming teams with a high trust quotient, thereby developing the loyalty to move quickly without hesitation - each member has each other's back. These types of relationships are dependable and rest on the ethics of a good relationship - the same one would hope to establish with their community of clients. Trust is a necessary ingredient in an increasingly virtual and volatile environment, especially in circumstances where management is separated by the globalized units we have now.

It is the manager's responsibility to promote team-building ideas and obtain buy-in from co-workers, not through leveraging their will under obligation but motivating them to succeed. It is also the manager's responsibility to bring out team-building skills in others. Manager's lacking the skills not only impede their own team but having nothing to teach or mentor – a predicament we see all to often today. If we see business as a collection of intentions, positive or negative, we can predict its outcomes based on those intentions. Remember the importance of developing a mission or 'intention' statement reflective of new values. Now the only question that need be asked is 'which ones does your organization promote or intend?'

As individuals we want work and labour to be a joy in life, bringing both prosperity and health and a sense of contribution to the larger systems of community and society. People want to have jobs they love that are both rewarding financially and satisfying the needs to express and be creative or analytical. A well-studied happiness survey suggests that people with an average salary of $60,000 per year are no less content than someone earning much more - only below that do people's life satisfaction drop with income. There is no joy in labour for those removed from the results. Working only for money is an abstract quest. Self-expression in work is only derived from the joy of building, selling and having a close relationship with those who would benefit from the work. If you take away the skills or trade, the ability to create and deliver the good, there is no longer any psychological reward for the work and unrest can occur.

With the need for organizations to change to reflect true sustainable development, people also need to reflect personal development and life satisfaction in their work. Now here is a twist. If an organization can keep its members healthy and happy, it may not need to pay more than $60,000 to anyone working there. They will stay regardless! Basic life needs will be met and a joy will return to the daily working life.

Jobs can no longer be the division of labour that marked the rise of the industrial age and perpetuate today. Looking at a few trends for socially improved workflow we can see:

- There will be less of our time 'in an office' because of communications technology and shared space
- There will be more active duties of stakeholder engagement and research building capacity for innovation
- There will be sponsored education – corporations may receive accreditation to deliver business degrees or diplomas allowing their employees to do Friday afternoons in class at work
- Flexible work times and negotiated schedules to allow for activities and family life
- Five-, four- and three-day work weeks dependent on lifestyles and apprentice programs
- Customizable benefits unique to individuals and family values. For example, a family may decide it does not want a drug plan but instead chooses to have that benefit towards a nutrition or yoga program

Reflecting the flexibility we desire in our work and personal lives will also be in our design. The future will be modular and adaptive. Just as parts of buildings and cars will be interchangeable we will embrace adaptivity.

Imagine what new buildings will look like if they reflect changing lifestyles. Walls can be moved and ratcheted back into place to create another space, or open one up with no de-construction. The conduits will already be pre-formed into energy converting walls in which to run wires, heating and water. Heating and cooling will be shared with the neighbours to save costs or eliminate them. Half the food will be grown on the outside walls of the building. Electric vehicles will be parked away from public space to enhance quality of streetscape, and much more. Business will need to think the same way, re-tooling its processes to provide these new functions because the future demands it. The windows will open!

Positive Psychology in the Workplace

It is my hope that the links between CSR, change management and sustainability have been made clear. The types of changes that need doing are actually happening right now, albeit slowly. It may require the next generation with their desire for flexibility and concerns for environment to fill the shoes of management and our political institutions before we address our real world issues. A new consciousness is needed in business and society to work with our issues with the environment and humanity.

To embrace becoming a new organization requires a transition in perceptions, attitudes and behaviours. Positive psychology will only grab hold if it is fostered and nourished. Creating an environment that recognises human needs will naturally lead to a type of sociability, improved relationships, and greater satisfaction. Engaging speakers capture our imaginations and intentions and frequently motivate to perform at a level that utilises our best talents. These types of speakers charge a lot of money and hold large venues of audiences filled with people looking for that special moment of realisation that they are part of something much larger and charismatic.

The premise for employee or community engagement is that they are not engaged. Sixty per cent of workers do not like their jobs. Communities struggle with understanding the economic or social planning that business and government undertake and the connections that it will have with their wellbeing. As life quickens, we are losing social skills and consideration for providing a conscientious and caring engagement process.

People do not leave bad jobs, they leave bad managers - it is the negative factors pushing people out, not the positive factors dragging people away. Disengaging with people is a process not an event. Just look at some of the main reasons people leave an organization: limited opportunity, lack do support and recognition, poor senior leadership/lack of skills, compensation, environment, space/time constraints. All of these are points that a CSR program can address and remedy.

Creating a place of work requires sustaining a culture of care. A sociable manager has the skills and experience to work with people, creating expectations based on reality, matching peoples values and skills to the job, and providing valuable feedback that builds the relationship. When employee turnover is just a cost of doing business, it's time to pack the bags.

It may seem far fetched that today's corporations could lead the way to a new type of collaborative socialism based on saving the planet, yet these organizations already have everything in place: a) an organized structure; b) a relationship with the stakeholders (communities, clients and shareholders); and c) a desire to invest wisely in the future. It is only the lack of innovation, political will and leadership that keeps our economy from transitioning to sustainable form of trade.

The most learned leaders with the ability to teach and open the minds of their peers are the most qualified for stewarding change. They will not just be leading a marketing department or holding hands with managers from task to task, but uniting workers, communities and stakeholders for a united cause that meshes with the mission of business and society. This is real leadership with the ability to create social change by doing business. It's happening today, in many parts of the globe, but perhaps not fast enough to keep communities from the economic upheaval, social disruption or environmental degradation.

To reach an enlightened agenda and begin to change the culture of the organization, the manager needs to be apprised of global conditions, the effects of pollution and waste, and the impact to the planet. These need to be on the dashboard of every CEO in every organization.

Only by seeing themselves as part of the whole, part of the earth's operating system, can they appreciate the everyday impacts of their decisions. This type of systems thinking can induce euphoria and a complexity that is astounding but perhaps unmanageable. To be a true corporate philosopher is to be able to communicate the connectedness of the business to natural processes and to create a purpose for the organization that transcends mere currency acquisition. He or she must lead their hearts and minds and in doing so will produce the most loyal and productive workforce possible.

Given the dire consequences of the cumulative impacts of our actions looming on the horizon, CSR could well be the primary and only function for a corporation or else risk everything. Logically, if we proceed in a polluting destructive manner, we will have to sacrifice health and security of future generations, which is extremely selfish and irresponsible. It is the selfishness and irresponsibility that CSR is addressing. If a business exists to create profit for shareholders, then a good business exists to create more goodness than just profit. With goodness in mind, we expand our business to include society and nature as these spheres that exist sometimes divided in our minds are in fact one and the same - a systems perspective of economy, society and environment.

Communities at work and at home are built on shared values. Our quest for learning and knowledge should be our greatest unifying goal - this is how things get better. We have only explored a few ways to acquire knowledge and information, but reason dictates that if we know so little about the planet that we continue to destroy it, then we need to learn much more and quickly. Business needs to have an interdisciplinary and integrative approach to developing value and this is where the opportunity lies - take away the reductionism and introduce people, systems and learning into the organization; a sort of business ecology if you will.

Maintaining a positive enriching climate to the organization may be difficult at times but this is where leadership is required. Do something unexpected to make people feel like they are part of something big and they are contributing. Take this momentum to the communities and stakeholders that are a part of the vision. Improve morale, wellbeing and passion. Anyone at any echelon of the organization can do this. If you have a supervisor or leader that is too unaware to change or allow this natural process to happen, prepare an exit plan. If you are a conscious human being and surrounded by dullards, this will do nothing for your own growth except develop your skills in patience. If you are a conscious leader, it is time you be the model you wish to see.

Research also shows that those who give most are not the wealthiest - they are the happiest. One of the greatest challenges of overcoming the industrial age methods of production will be to resolve the tension between organizational needs and self-actualization. What industrialisation did was to build a scientific method to production, dividing process into little parts to produce more, faster, until the big picture was lost. This reductionism is still prevalent in science and management today and is perhaps the largest problem to overcome in terms of how we think about problem solving.

Only with a shift in thinking will we initiate a new era for economy and society. Indeed change in a seemingly radical way, may cause doubt and fear, however change will either be implemented with our careful consideration or forced upon us depending on timing and preparedness. Although people may be comfortable 'liking' pages or tweeting links to good works, in the end, that's not going to cut it. All good intentions are coupled with an equal and congruent action in the physical universe. We need action and there is no action without obtaining information, feedback and learning.

Action learning (AL) is a technique that utilises questions, knowledge and reflection. It is much like appreciative inquiry (AI) but is less visionary and more focused on specific problem solving. Like AI, it still requires inquiry, examining human potential, collaboration, authenticity, a systemic view, and committed participation. AL focuses on organization level issues that are crucial and complex, the solving of which will create a meaningful organizational change.

Larry Wilson, successful entrepreneur and founder of the Wilson Learning Corporation, has worked with a number of business and global leaders. His insights gained highlight four new characteristics emerging in the business world and reveal that indeed business culture is learning and changing.

The Four Factors

Trust

"Fear and the inability to trust are two of the most important limiting factors for executives" (Harman, 1996). Clearly, as a society in fear, we paralyse our ability to think, take action and cease to move towards our potentialities. We must realize that it is a choice we make that determines the path ahead. Living in fear, darkens the path, removes purpose and thus freedom. It is trust that allows communities and nations to come together to co-create a brighter future. It allows for us to depend on each other and develop a faith in humankind. Depending on whether one has fear or feeling of trust, the resulting worldview will be much different and so will all choices made as a result.

Purpose

Part of the journey of being a human being is discovering our purpose. The closer we align to something that reflects our intrinsic values, the more we are driven to self-actualize. Self-actualization is a learning activity. We learn about ourselves by learning about others, their plights, their successes and their journeys. We derive purpose from understanding our role within our communities – this creates identity and belonging, the security necessary to safely move emotionally beyond insecurity. Discovering one's own potential for higher order thinking and creativity builds within us a problem solver and a source of wisdom. This transition to a teacher role later in life is essential for the sustainability of youth who rely on transfer of wisdom and knowledge to survive physically and emotionally.

Creating a sense of purpose for people is one of the most powerful motivators in humanity.

Creating a Vision

I've previously discussed the importance of having, intending, affirming and acting on a vision. Believing and being the vision brings legitimacy to the organization and a path to future prosperity. We examine the past to understand the future. We repeat events from our past with great clarity, often the negative one's, both in mind and in unconscious actions. Having a clear positive vision solidifies purpose. If the vision is shared among a group of people, it can be even more powerful. The vision must be understood and shared amongst the group's value system. Those who do not believe in it will not participate for whatever reason. But how could someone not want to be part of developing a happier, more productive and healthy society? How can anyone not want to be a part of that experience?

Acting with Feedback

We learn, we do, we observe and we change. The basic tenet of progress and yet so many people seem to be stuck in the do and do again expecting different results. Break the static loops.

Utilizing Affirmations

Studies show that high performing athletes use visualization techniques to success. They see with their mind's eye a desired future state and affirm these goals to themselves. This helps to structure the brain in such a way as to prepare and condition it. Using visualizations and affirmations also forms a relationship with many factors in the environment. The conditions of success become dependent on seeing oneself in harmony within a particular setting. This is where such tools as neuro-linguistics and cognitive therapy become valuable.

Utilizing vision and adjusting neural activity taps into a part of the consciousness that is little if not altogether ignored in business acumen, yet fully acceptable as therapy on a personal basis. This

167

separation of business from the meta-physical or spiritual values compromises ethics that people may bring to work but under obligation status may never express. The business vision statement should read as an affirmation of organizational values. The over arching question to management is whether the leadership reflects the ethics behind the statement and the workplace environment genuinely supports or affirms those values.

Motivation manifests itself when either a person is deviated from their identifiable norm and they self-regulate to achieve balance or they seek to avoid pain or attract pleasure. We can see that most economic rationale; the selling of goods and services, is based on motivating hedonism. This also works for other points of progress.

On Spirituality and the Workplace

Spirituality has remained a conceptual and esoteric topic with little understanding to the world of business. If we take spirituality to mean the feeling and belief of connectedness through life, living and thus consciousness, we can see how spiritual values are those represented by organizational benefits such as increased commitment and morale, creativity, greater compassion, trust, and ethical behaviour, personal and professional growth; enhanced team and community building and increased ability to cope with change and uncertainty.

Spirituality- Originating from the Latin word *spirare,* which means "to breathe," spirituality is represented as a life force, "traditionally believed to be the vital principle or animating force within living beings".

Another definition is equally applicable and more comprehensible: "A worldview plus a path to achieve it" (Cavanaugh, 2002). In this definition, we can now view spirituality globally, across religions and personal beliefs, combined with purpose. Virtues, morals, and habits fall out of one's worldview and sense of purpose. A lack of meaning can perpetuate in a workplace if the organization is deemed separate from the rest of one's life. Spirituality in the workplace is not to be confused with institutionalized religion, cheerleading or speech making to motivate employees. These oppressive and cosmetic bursts are short lived and do not reach the hearts of people and in the long-term and risk alienating workers from management. Rather a more productive approach is to connect with employees on meaningful and common themes.

Spirituality is often viewed as connectedness to one's environment including other people and their environments. Good socialization and integrity lead to innovation, trust and commitment, values that cannot be bought with reward systems. Looking at a systematic way to examine virtue in the workplace can also identify corruptive factors that demotivate and cause turnover in employee retention. Developing a spiritual approach to workplace management is a positive and demonstrable way to reinforce the mission (affirmation), values and commitment of the company to the betterment of society and the planet.

Spirituality can simply be 'the right thing to do'. A good attitude and commitment to employees will result in decisions that support and nurture their development and provide an atmosphere of security and trust. Having virtues of prudence and courage can have no other effect than to consider the future wellbeing of others and thus is a more sustainable outcome. In this way, spirituality is the deepening of relationships.

This may not be something spelled out in doctrines, but rather in the treatment of people and the purview of leadership – simply demonstrating the taking of responsibility in deeds leads to legitimacy. How many people follow leaders with spiritual values? Can you think of any historical figures? Authors? Are people paid to follow them or do they do so because those leaders resonate their own values?

Conclusion

"Managers will either learn to optimise the system, or go out of business" – W. Edward Deming

In an age of scepticism and relativism, we are surely left short with unifying things to believe in. Were there one single absolute truth, one thing we could gather round and believe in, we might be able to muster our knowledge and leverage our resourcefulness to create a better world for all. But we remain divided. Our environment is one such totem. More than that, nature is within the fabric of our being, undeniably, scientifically, spiritually, artistically and justifiably, it is the basis for all of our quality of life. Business is simply the organizational mechanism to convert and exchange resources. So why then is business at odds with its own source of revenue and well being?

There is no doubt we are in an age of great transition and big decision making. The quality of the transition and the wisdom of the decision will be dependent on the best of ourselves being involved, not the decision itself. I believe there will be big decisions made by society - not government or business - that will change the course of history. These decisions may not even be a choice but recognizing simply that we need to change our behaviours.

Why not rise to the occasion in the times of our greatest challenge and present ourselves to history as the people who created a better world? We can choose to be different, be better and leave the planet in a better state than we found it.

Although the term 'sustainability' has become cliché to the point that it simply means continuing the status quo despite greater challenges, it could not be farther from the truth. Sustainability also does not mean environmentalism although it does mean having an environmental conscience. Sustainability is and will always be about our relationship to the environment.

Environmentalism has been around since the beginning of time and has always been expressed through culture, community and science. The feeling of connectedness with our surroundings is environmentalism. Many cultures have evolved since the dawn of civilization to express this connectedness, which sadly, has been steamrolled by growing self-indulgence and cultural ignorance. Sustainability is about recognising our place in environmentalism, our impacts and our consciousness about what the earth, our only home, is going through because of our actions.

Growing sustainably will not be a product of making deals but a product of foresight and inclusivity with an organization's stakeholders. The future belongs to those who create and lead the change, those left in the establishment of old will be swept away and be left in whatever toxic mess is left behind. Sustainable development is only making progress if it is oriented toward a better society and includes everyone. There is no sense in economic production if you sacrifice health and community.

We can now understand how instituting a cultural change within the organization can bring an ethical context that will motivate and support employees in their own personal performance and as a result, financial performance and environmental consciousness. Social capital is necessary for fostering knowledge, the kind of knowledge management practices and team dynamics that makes cooperative action possible.

By cooperating we can achieve much more than we could alone. Remember, this is a cardinal rule in systems thinking, that emergent properties are only possible when all the parts work together in harmony - it is the same in nature. Managers need to be coached in such matters and understand that they are psychologists first and gang masters second.

Human beings are not as productive when fostered to be individualistic as opposed to synergistic. Any organizational tools or reward systems that promote individual performance above the others will create a pathological team atmosphere. Managers need to be educated to the needs of people and society to be truly enlightened and develop those people skills necessary to enhancing performance. Managers will also need to administer to any old structures that unnecessarily restrict flexibility and autonomy and project manage with sets of new performance indicators.

Thriving in the long-term, the economy will transition to a closed loop, zero net impact model. One person's waste will be another person's treasure or else risk being another person's nightmare, which has traditionally become a social justice issue and a reputation breaker for many businesses. The goal for all organizations must be to network with other organizations to see where the connections can be made to maximize industrial ecological processes and derive the greatest benefits for the partnership - a true win-win-win.

A new culture of awareness is on the horizon and new priorities around a post-industrial age, creating a consistency in behaviour, will yield benefits to health and community. The education system will need to reflect the type of managers we need for the future, thinking holistically and with the appropriate people skills. The environment already knows what to do, it is only humans that are still striving for that answers and therefore it is us that must change, not the world.

The consumer ethic that exists now demands the separation of human consciousness from nature in order to divest an individual from the impacts of their actions - to blind them to the troubles we cause. In contrast, the interaction of human and natural systems is now the study of sustainable development.

Organizations, whether public or private, represent our group efforts towards a common goal. We form them because we can do more together than apart. Our working lives take up most of our productive waking hours, and direct our energy toward these organizational goals. It would be a shame as a society to continue in the vein of working towards despair or self-interest, reducing our advancement toward social justice, optimum health and happiness and letting down the youth today by taking their tomorrow. There is much more potential than just materialism when people are organized for a larger purpose. Let it happen.

Good people deserve quality of life, which includes material means, comfort and security. Once these are met, an individual can seek the highest pursuits of human existence whether in the arts, sciences or philosophy. The greatest advancements in humankind came when resources were available for us to explore and discover how things work and how they came to be. We need to take responsibility for the consumption of those resources. This exploration created paradigm shifts in thinking and altered worldviews. Perpetuating systems that keep resources in the hands of the few is ultimately confining our species and will result in a dark age.

Progress is constantly working towards creating those same revelational experiences but we need those same conditions to prosper and that can only be done if we are healthy and there are enough resources. If we become too distracted or too busy to contemplate progress then we adopt reactive models of behaviour and ride a sinking ship with no direction. Business and public institutions are not exempt from the same responsibility for exploration into sustainable development. Already we are distracted to the point where we are forgetting what we have forgotten, who we are, where we come from.

Sustainability must aim to more than just sustenance. If personal and organisational advancement becomes only an option for the few, we have missed the point of sustainability. Positive paradigm shifts will occur when knowledge can be shared under fair and unrestricted conditions, creating the potential for greater self-sufficiency and innovation. We now have seven billion minds on the planet. Should we not foster all of them in hopes just one could propose an idea to change the world for the better? If we envision what a sustainable work life balance would be in future we would probably include:

- A better understanding of time and energy restrictions on human stress levels
- A focus on prevention rather than cures to problems
- Flexibility for families to take care of their children at home, maintaining the crucial structure of love and respect necessary for a child's proper development
- A flexible work week to avoid congestion and stress, leaving time for volunteerism and community activities while space for interns and cooperative programs
- Services in the workplace that include day care, therapeutic needs, local supply and food production, a gymnasium, and accredited university courses to induce continuous learning

- Retreats that are actually retreating to our spiritual roots and connections with each other and the land
- Managers that must step through rites of passage to demonstrate their emotional intelligence and mentoring capacity to guide and develop people into successful team and community members
- Urban areas free of congestion, pollution and limits to development densities

There is no reason why the corporation cannot aim for profit and making the world a better place. It is all right to dream of Utopia: it gives us a direction and we feel a purpose but we must feel it in our hearts or we fall prey to rationalizing our dreams. A careful inspection of the above points will show these changes are all within our capability now. We can make life better in a flash, the rest requires long term plans.

Administering the above types of practices may seem esoteric, but when you consider that the current life-work-style is contributing to stress, heart disease and diabetes, dysfunctional family structures, then a fundamental change in re-defining productivity has to happen. Until organizational structures become a deliberative and participative forum that can decide how the organization (and consequently society) will function, the manager must be held accountable for the function and quality of working life for his or her team members. Ultimately the general direction must be led from the top.

What are the consequences of not transitioning to a healthy society? We are already experiencing the problems of global pollution. There are unidentified substances in our blood streams, increases in cancer, diabetes, and disease rates in young and old. Expect a massive drop in biodiversity and key species going extinct as is the case now. With climate change, it may get so bad that hunger and water shortage will create strife even among the middle and upper classes of North America. A rise in unemployment will occur because of inflation and greed and people acting our of fear for lack of security. This is happening right now in different regions around the globe.

Basically if we do not alter our thinking about how to approach our business activities, we will only be using our conscious and most creative waking hours to turn the machine until it runs out of oil. Then it will be everyone for themselves. No more time or resources to create or leisure, just living day to day not knowing where next weeks meals will be coming from. There is no winning, strategy or purpose to the types of activities that continue to pollute our minds and the planet.

I have shown the importance of changing mindset and for considering wellbeing. Purpose and meaning in one's work provide motivation and commitment, driving the corporate results. All people know the joy of working towards something they believe in – it is no longer work, it becomes a vocation, a dedication. I write of transitioning business to a solution-oriented organization and using CSR as a tool to assist change. These ethics of commitment and consideration are needed if humanity is to survive into the next age, past the pollution and inequality. We have created marvels and developed technologies previously undreamed. We have reinvented ourselves several times throughout history. Time is of the essence. We can do so again.

> The purpose of a business firm is not simply to make profit, but is found in its existence as a community of persons who in various ways are endeavouring to satisfy their basic needs and who form a particular group at the service of the whole of society. Profit is a regulator of the life of a business, but it is not the only one; other human and moral factors must also be considered, which in the long term are at least equally important for the life of a business. – *Pope J. Paul II, The Hundredth Year*

References

Abou-Zeid, E.-S. (2008). Knowledge management and business strategies: theoretical frameworks and empirical research. Hershey: Information Science Reference.

Adler, R. B., & Rodman, G. R. (1997). Understanding human communication (6th ed.). Fort Worth: Harcourt Brace College Publishers.

Amy, A. H. (2008). Leaders as facilitators of individual and organizational learning. Leadership & Organization Development Journal, 29(3), 212.

Andreadis, N. (2009). Learning and organizational effectiveness: a systems perspective. Performance Improvement, 48(1).

Baldry, C., & Hallier, J. (2010). Welcome to the House of Fun: Work Space and Social Identity. Democracy Economic and Industrial 31(1), 150-172.

Barber, B. R. (2007). Con how markets corrupt children, infantilize adults, and swallow citizens whole (1st ed.). New York: W.W. Norton & Co.

Berc, J., Cameron, S., Cordle, S., Crosby, M., Martin, L., Norton, D., et al. (1998). The ecosystem approach: science and information management issues, gaps and needs (Vol. 40): Elsevier Science.

Bertalanffy, L. v., & Laszlo, E. (1972). The Relevance of general systems theory; papers presented to Ludwig von Bertalanffy on his seventieth birthday. New York: G. Braziller.

Bhattacharya, C., Sen, S., & Korschun, D. (2008). Using Corporate Social Responsibility to Win the War for Talent. MIT Sloan Management Review, 49(2), 37-44.

Boiral, O. (2009). Greening the Corporation Through Organizational Citizenship Behaviours. Journal of Business Ethics, 87(2), 221.

Brundtland, G. H., & World Commission on Environment and Development. (1987). Our Common Future. Oxford ; New York: Oxford University Press.

Bugliarello, G. (2006). Urban sustainability: Dilemmas, challenges and paradigms. 28(1-2), 19-26.

Cabrera, D., Colosi, L., & Lobdell, C. (2008). Systems Thinking. Evaluation and Program Planning, 31, 299-310.

Cavanagh, G. F., & Bandsuch, M. R. (2002). Virtue as a benchmark for spirituality in business. Journal of Business Ethics, 38(1/2), 109-117.

Chan, S. Y. S. (2009). New Green Tax Incentive in Hong Kong. International Tax Journal, 35(6), 55-69.

Chatterji, A., & Levine, D. (2006). Breaking down the wall of codes: Evaluating non-financial performance measurement. California Management Review, 48(2).

Chida, Y., & Steptoe, A. (2008). Positive psychological wellbeing and mortality: a quantitative review of prospective observational studies. Psychosom Med., 70(7), 741-756.

Cross, R., Thomas, R., & Light, D. (2009). How 'Who You Know' Affects What You Decide. MIT Sloan Management Review, 50(2), 35-42.

Curkovic, S., & Sroufe, R. (2006). Total quality environmental management and total cost assessment: An exploratory study. International journal of production economics, 105, 560-579.

Daft, R. L., & Lengel, R. H. (1986). Organizational Information Requirements, Media Richness And Structural Design. Management Science, 32(5), 554-571.

Davis, A., & Blass, E. (2007). The Future Workplace: Views from the floor. Futures, 39, 38-52.

Delre, S., Jager, W., Bijmolt, T., & Janssen, M. (2010). Will It Spread or Not? The Effects of Social Influences and Network Topology on Innovation Diffusion. The Journal of Product Innovation Management, 27(2).

Desouza, K. C., & Hensgen, T. (2005). Managing information in complex organizations : semiotics and signals, complexity and chaos. Armonk, N.Y.: M.E. Sharpe.

Durning, A. (1992). How Much Is Enough?: The Consumer Society and the Future of the Earth. New York: W. W. Norton & Company Ltd.

Ehin, C. (2009). The Organizational Sweet Spot: Engaging the Innovative Dynamics of Your Social Networks.

Ehrenfeld, J. R. (2004). Searching for Sustainability: No Quick Fix. Reflections, 5(8).

Elmes, M., Gemmill, G. (1990). The Psychodynamics and Mindlessness in Dissent in Small Groups. Small Group Research. 21(1), 28-44

Funk, K. (2003). Sustainability and Performance. MIT sloan Management Review.

Elm, D., & Nichols, M. L. 1993. An investigation of the moral reasoning of managers. Journal of Business Ethics, 12: 817-833.

Guidice, R. M., Heames, J. T., & Wang, S. (2009). The indirect relationship between organizational-level knowledge worker turnover and innovation. The Learning Organization, 16(2), 143-167.

Hamel, G., & Prahalad, C. K. (1994). Competing for the future. Boston, Mass.: Harvard Business School Press.

Harman, W. (1998). Global Mind Change. Institute for Noetic Sciences

Harmon, K. (2009, December 16). Bugs Inside: What Happens When the Microbes That Keep Us Healthy Disappear? Scientific American.

Hart, S. L., Milstein, M. B., & Caggiano, J. (2003). Creating Sustainable Value. The Academy of Management Executive, 17(2), 56-69.

Harvard business review on the persuasive leader. (2008). Boston: Harvard Business School Pub.

Hawken, P., Lovins, A. B., & Lovins, H. (1999). Natural capitalism : creating the next industrial revolution (1st ed.). Boston: Little, Brown and Co.

Henriques, I., & Sadorsky, P. (1999). The relationship between environmental commitment and managerial perceptions of stakeholder importance. Academy of Management Journal, 42(1), 87-99.

Homer-Dixon, T. F. (2000). The ingenuity gap. New York ; Toronto: Knopf.

Kohlberg, L. (1969). Stage and sequence. The cognitive developmental approach to socialization. In D. A. Goslin (Ed.), Handbook of socialization theory: 347-480. Chicago: Rand McNally.

Kotler, P., & Lee, N. (2005). Corporate Social Responsibility: Doing the most good for your company and cause: Wiley.

Mainelli, M. (2004). Ethical volatility: how CSR ratings and returns might be changing the world of risk. Balance Sheet, 12(1), 42-46.

Maon, F., Lindgreen, A., & Swaen, V. (2009). Designing and Implementing Corporate Social Responsibility: An Integrative Framework Grounded in Theory and Practice. Journal of Business Ethics, 87(71).

Margolis, J. D., Elfenbein, H. A., & Walsh, J. P. (2007, August). Does it pay to be good? A meta-analysis and redirection of research on the relationship between corporate social and financial performance. Paper presented at the Presentation at the Academy of Management Meetings Philadelphia, PA.

Maslow, A. H., Stephens, D. C., Heil, G., & Maslow, A. H. (1998). Maslow on management. New York: John Wiley.

McLean, J. (2009). A place for Creativity in Management? The British Journal of Administrative Management, 30-31.

Mitchell, R. K., Agle, B. R., & Wood, D. J. (1997). Toward a theory of stakeholder identification and salience: Defining the principle of who and what really counts. Academy of Management Review.

Montano, B. R., & Dillon, R. (2005). The Impact of Technology on Relationships within Organizations. Information Technology and Management, 6(2-3), 227.

Mulvihill, P. R., & Milan, M. J. (2007). Subtle world: beyond sustainability, beyond information. Futures, 39(6), 657(612).

Nahapiet, J., Gratton, L., & Rocha, H. (2005). Knowledge and relationships: when cooperation is the norm. European Management Review, 2, 3-14.

Nawrocka, D., & Parker, T. (2009). Finding the connection: environmental management systems and environmental performance. Journal of Cleaner Production, 17, 601-607.

Nord, W., & Fuller, S. (2009). Increasing Corporate Social Responsibility Through an Employee-centered Approach. Employee Responsibilities and Rights Journal, 21(4), 279.

Nwankwo, E., Phillips, N., & Tracey, P. (2007). Social Investment through Community Enterprise: The Case of Multinational Corporations Involvement in the Development of Nigerian Water Resources. Journal of Business Ethics, 73(1), 91-102.

Oberg, C., & Grundstrom, C. (2009). Challenges and opportunities in innovative firms' network development. International Journal of Innovation Management, 13(4), 593-613.

OCC. (2006). Stern Review: The Economics of Climate Change: Cambridge University Press.

Organ, D., Podsakoff, P., & MacKenzie, S. (2006). Organizational Citizenship Behaviour: Its Nature, Antecedents, and Consequences.

Pacey, A. (1994). The Culture of Technology. Cambridge: The MIT Press.

Pastoriza, D., Arino, M. A., & Ricart, J. E. (2009). Creating an Ethical Work Context: A Pathway to Generate Social Capital in the Firm. Journal of Business Ethics, 88, 477-489.

Peloza, J., & Falkenberg, L. (2009). The Role of Collaboration in Achieving Corporate Social Responsibility Objectives. California Management Review, 51(3).

Petri, H. L. (1986). Motivation: Theory and research (2nd ed.). Belmont, CA: Wadsworth.

Pidd, M. (2004). Systems modelling : theory and practice. Chichester, England ; Hoboken, NJ: John Wiley & Sons.

Porter, M., & Kramer, M. (2006). Strategy & Society: The Link Between Competitive Advantage and Corporate Social Responsibility. Harvard Business Review, 84(12), 78-92.

Prahalad, C. K., & Hamel, G. (1990). The core competence of the corporation. Harvard Business Review, May-June.

Rosa, J. A., Qualis, W. J., & Fuentes, C. (2008). Involving mind, body, and friends: Management that engenders creativity. Journal of Business Research, 61(6), 631-639.

Schermerhorn, J. R. (2008). Management ([9th ed.). Hoboken, NJ: J. Wiley.

Seitanidi, M. M. (2008). Adaptive Responsibilities: Nonlinear Interactions in Cross Sector Social Partnerships Adaptive Responsibilities, 10(3), 51-64.

Shuili, D., Bhattacharya, C. B., & Sankar, S. Maximizing Business Returns to Corporate Social Responsibility (CSR): The Role of CSR Communication. International Journal of Management Reviews, 12(1), 8-19.

Sniderman, P. R., & Nelson, D. L. (2007). Managing organizational behaviour in Canada. Toronto: Thomson Nelson.

Sosa, R., & Gero, J. (2008). Social structures that promote change in a complex world: The complementary roles of strangers and acquintances in innovation. Futures, 40, 577-585.

Stajkovic, A. D., & Luthans, F. (2003). Behavioural Management and Task Performance in Organizations: Conceptual Background, Meta-analysis, and Test of Alternative Models. Personnel Psychology, 56(Spring).

Trevino, L., Weaver, G., Reynolds, S. (2006). Behavioural Ethics in Organizations: A Review. Journal of Management (December 2006), 32 (6), pg. 951-990.

Vitell, J., Singhapakdi, A., Thomas, J. (2001). Consumer ethics: an application and empirical testing of the Hunt-Vitell theory of ethics. Journal Of Consumer Marketing, Vol. 18 No. 2, pp. 153-178.

Waddock, S., & McIntosh, M. (2009). Beyond Corporate Responsibility: Implications for Management Development. Business and Society Review, 114(3), 295-325.

Waldman, J. D. (2007). Thinking Systems Need Systems Thinking. Systems Research and Behavioural Science, 24, 271-284.

Wilber, K. (1997). The eye of spirit : an integral vision for a world gone slightly mad. Boston: Shambhala.

Wood, D. J. (1991). Corporate social performance revisited. Academy of Management Review, 16, 691-718.

Wood, D. J. (2010). Measuring Corporate Social Performance: A Review. International Journal of Management Reviews, 12(1), 50-84.

www.ingramcontent.com/pod-product-compliance
Lightning Source LLC
Chambersburg PA
CBHW020202200326
41521CB00005BA/224